YASHIM COOKS
ISTANBUL

YASHIM COOKS
ISTANBUL

JASON GOODWIN

ARGONAUT

CONTENTS

INTRODUCTION

When I started to write *The Janissary Tree*, the first of Yashim's five adventures set in Ottoman Istanbul, I had no idea that Yashim would turn out to be a cook. He was the sultan's investigator, he had a poignant disability, and the Janissaries – the crack Ottoman infantry – were about to make trouble. Those, I thought, were all the ingredients I needed for a thriller.

But the cooking came through. I first reached the city on foot, hiking for months from the Baltic coast, and I still can't think of Istanbul without dreaming of food. Each day on the walk brought us some new foretaste of Istanbul: stronger coffee, a minaret, orthodox domes, bright printed cottons, or the eastern rhythm of gypsy music. But only when we reached The City did we discover what it was to eat well. After months of plain fare, we ate fish in a restaurant suspended under the old Galata bridge, watching the ferries come and go. We ate mutton and aubergine wrapped in a paper parcel in the Grand Bazaar. Bread of exceptional freshness appeared at every table. Cauldrons bubbled, full of sweet or spicy vegetable stews, with morsels of tender lamb spitted and roasted over the charcoal braziers whose scent drifted through the air. On the shores of the Golden Horn we ate mackerel sandwiches, the fish just taken from the Bosphorus, filleted and grilled on the boats. After months of soviet-style scarcity and monotony, Istanbul was like a gingerbread house.

The Ottoman kitchen

It had its fairy-tale palace, too. Set on the first of the city's seven hills, overlooking the Bosphorus and the Asian coast, Topkapi was home to the Ottoman sultans from the fifteenth to the nineteenth century. Neither a castle, nor a stately home, its courtyards and kiosks created an encampment in stone, a collection of fossilised tents and open spaces. A wit once remarked that it looked as if it had been shaken out of a bag. In olden days the rows of immobile janissaries standing guard around the walls of the Court, the silent servants, the bowing slaves, bore witness to the sultan's absolute authority.

The Ottoman architect Mimar Sinan built the palace kitchens in the 1570s. They are just a series of domed rooms, but outside you can count the ten pairs of massive chimneys. Once there were pantries, store-rooms, and offices for the team of clerks who kept meticulous records of what was bought, and how much was spent. Hundreds of men lived and worked here, feeding as many as ten thousand people in a day. The soup, pilaf, helva, vegetable dishes, meats, breads, pastries were produced by master chefs with as many as a hundred apprentices. They had their own dormitories, a fountain, a mosque, and a hammam where they could bathe.

Stupendous quantities of food came into the palace. In 1723 the butcher's bill listed thirty thousand head of beef, sixty thousand sheep, twenty thousand veal calves, ten thousand kids, and two hundred thousand fowl. Half a million bushels of chickpeas. Twelve thousand pounds of salt. The palace tore through food like the city that surrounded it. In 1581 eight ships from Egypt brought enough grain to feed the city for a single day.

The Ottoman larder

Istanbul stood at the confluence of trade routes across an empire that stretched from the Balkans to Egypt, and from the borders of Georgia to the Adriatic. To its soldiers, and its shepherds, it was an empire of mountains – the Balkans, the Rhodopes, the Pindus, the Taurus, the Nur, the Pontic Alps, the Caucasus, the Hejaz, the Lebanon and Anti-Lebanon, among others. The food trade followed the winds that buffeted the empire's coasts – the dry summer Meltemi or Etesian of the Aegean islands; the cool Gregale; the oppressive Khamsin of Egypt, and its grim Simoom; the icy Kosava of Serbia; the rough afternoon Lodos that chops at the Aegean, like the northerly Maestro, cousin to the French Mistral; the Bora of the Adriatic; the damp Levant; and the Sirocco whipping up the tides in Venice, known in the Balkans as Jugo, and on Malta cryptically as Xlokk.

Egypt was the Ottoman's granary. Anatolia was their fruit-bowl. The mountain pastures of Europe and Asia provided them with sweet mutton and cheese. Every region had its speciality, like the delicate and delicious trout of Lake Ohrid on the border between Macedonia and Albania, which were carried overland, live, to Topkapi palace for the sultan's feasts. The best of everything arrived there in its season - watermelon and green onions from Bursa, figs from the Aegean coast, fruit from the Black Sea. Vegetables came from market gardens snuggled up beneath the ancient Byzantine walls, and different districts of the city became famous for certain products, like the clotted cream of Eyup, or the flaky pastries of Karakoy. The garlic came from Izmit, lemons from Mersin, cheeses in skins from the mountains of Moldavia. An imperial palace, in a city of imperial

appetite, produced a cookery defined along with the Chinese and the French as one of the three great food cultures of the world.

As the preface to Turabi Efendi's *Turkish Cookery*, first published in 1864, says: 'Ottoman cuisine is a rich cornucopia comprised of Balkan, Aegean, Caucasian, Syrian, Lebanese and Anatolian cuisines combined in a single kettle.'

Eating in Istanbul

Food sizzled on the street, simmered in the palace. The grandest of markets was the Egyptian bazaar, right on the waters of Golden Horn, whose stones still leak the scents of ambergris and coriander. Every district had its market, and fish were sold fresh from the deep waters of the Bosphorus, not to mention the anchovies which, along the Black Sea coast, had something of a religious flavour, and were used even to make bread.

All this required cooking – but you didn't ever have to cook yourself, because the streets not only teemed with people from every corner of the world – Greeks and Turks, of course, Armenians and Jews, Laz and Georgians, Serbs, Arabs and the odd Frank – but with wandering peddlers, and fast food shacks. Rigorously patrolled by the kadis, who exacted summary punishment for infringement of the rules, these street vendors were even unwittingly patronised by sultans, who might wander incognito through the streets (Osman III liked roasted chickpeas, kebabs, and a sort of buttered toast called gözleme). Today you can still buy roasted chestnuts, or stuffed mussels, or stop a simit-seller for a ring of bread like a pretzel.

Thirsty, you beckoned the sherbert seller, the waterman, the orange juice vendor, each with his tank, and his tube, his glasses and his tray, and his unique patter and paraphernalia. Food could mean gossip and friendship, meze prepared for an evening of conversation over raki, little bowls laid out with a handful of black olives and a cucumber nudging the salt – or the full blown array of carefully prepared dishes, no warmer than the evening air.

Meze include the dishes called dolma, meaning stuffed; stuffed vine leaves – dolmades – from Greece are well-known. The Ottomans would stuff anything, from a mackerel to a leek. The New World vegetables which are now the staple of any Mediterranean kitchen did not become widespread until the early 19th century; nor for the most part did the Turks cook with oil, preferring butter or even mutton fat – the repertoire still contains a number of dishes, usually served as meze, which are cooked specifically *à l'huile d'olive*.

The sultan, by tradition, fed his people. Public kitchens served pilaff to the poor, and the year proceeded with a round of public feasts, linked to religious ceremonies like the night of the Prophet's birth or the end of Ramadan, not to mention innumerable celebration feasts for imperial circumcisions and weddings.

The Ottoman empire collapsed after World War I, but ways of cooking in this part of the world have not changed as radically as its political arrangements. Ottoman traditions still underpin the cookery of Albania as of Lebanon, Greece as well as Turkey.

How to use this book

And so Yashim became a cook, as well as a sleuth. He is, as readers will know, the sultan's confidential agent. No doors are closed to him, not even the doors of the harem.

The recipes in this book are inspired by the novels, where some of them first appear. When Yashim entertains his friend Palewski, Polish ambassador to the Sublime Porte, to dinner, he invites readers into the half-lost world of 19th century Istanbul. His digressions into food reveal the city and the civilisation surrounding it, down to the spices that scent the air of the Egyptian Bazaar. How better to evoke Ottoman multiculturalism now than by eating our way around it?

People have said that they taste Istanbul in the novels. So I have interwoven the recipes with snatches of Yashim's stories, for flavour of a different sort, and taken the opportunity to illustrate not only recipes but also some of the familiar sights of Yashim's world.

Cooks come in all sorts, like the occasions they cater to. Some will use recipes as a reminder and an inspiration, boldly forging their own versions according to temperament, preference and what's in the larder. Others cleave faithfully to the text. What works so easily for a casual lunch might be stress-inducing for a formal dinner, but everyone should be encouraged to go off piste now and then. I've suggested some variations and adaptations, but most of the recipes in this book are open to interpretation. Experiment to the limits of your imagination. Substitute dill for parsley, add coriander seed or a hot fresh chilli, and you won't do yourself, your friends or the dish any harm. This isn't an exercise in historical re-enactment, it's about eating well, the way you like; which is just why Palewski always comes to Yashim's flat for Thursday dinner.

If you already know the Yashim stories, I hope the pictures and the passages from the novels will remind you fondly of his adventures, and illustrate his Istanbul world. Many things have changed in Istanbul since the 1840s, though surprisingly much remains the same. Some of the pictures recall an age of considerable grace and decorative beauty, which belong to the arts of life, to skill and good taste honed to one sort of perfection down the centuries. I hope you will enjoy the texts like a selection of meze, set out for flavour and texture. The Ottoman world was often riven by violence and injustice, and the end game is not yet quite played out, but it was also beautiful and sufficient in most places, and at most times.

Its food, like its arts, are a continuing gift.

The recipes come in rough order of appearance, rather than being divided as meat/fish/vegetables/dessert. The Ottoman served their meals that way, in a blizzard of dishes big and small. Unless otherwise stated, the recipes here are for four people.

On ingredients

Most of the ingredients in this book need no introduction: they are refreshingly ordinary. Istanbul, after all, is a city of pronounced seasonality, making use of common winter vegetables like squash and carrots as well as the more delicate exotics. Seasonality means fresh, very fresh.

As we go to print, the fate of the 1500 year old Yedikule Gardens, the mother of all urban farms, hangs in the balance. Famed for their lettuce, as well as peas and tomatoes, these market gardens under the massive walls of old Constantinople have been tilled since early Byzantine days. They are threatened by the municipality, which wants to turn them into a park, with paths.

The Ottomans were more adventurous with their spices than modern Turks: after all, they were rich and powerful and held the gorgeous Middle East in fee, not to mention the Black Sea and the Balkans. The overland spice routes into Europe wound through the Egyptian Bazaar in Istanbul.

Two kinds of hot pepper are worth tracking down. *Kırmızı*, or *pul biber* often sits on the table beside the salt, to sprinkle over your kebab or soup. A common variety is known in the West as Aleppo pepper. *Isot*, or *Urfa*, biber is more subtle, made from red Urfa peppers that grow to deep purple. After harvesting they are dried in the sun by day but wrapped up at night the better to concentrate their flavour, which is smoky, slightly sweet, and deliciously warm. It registers nowhere on the Scoville scale but once you have tried isot biber you may find it compulsive.

Sumac is easily sourced. It's a wild berry with a curiously good lemony and slightly sour taste. As an ingredient it predates the lemon in Turkey.

I urge you to grow lots of flat leaf parsley, mint and dill, which are traditional 'warming' herbs, as well as oregano, and sage. There is nothing sadder than a sprig of herbs when a bunch would do. It is positively un-Ottoman. And while most of these recipes specify precise quantities, bear in mind the fate of Empress Eugenie's personal chef.

> The French emperor Napoleon III and his empress, Eugenie, spent a week in Istanbul as the Sultan's guests in 1862. The Empress was so taken with a concoction of aubergine puree and lamb that she asked for permission to send her own chef to the kitchens to study the recipe. The request was graciously granted by their host, and the chef duly set off with his scales and notebook. The Sultan's cook slung him out, roaring, 'An imperial chef cooks with his feelings, his eyes, and his nose!
>
> *Lords of the Horizons: A History of the Ottoman Empire.*

It is less well known that Sultan Abdulmecid II courteously presented Eugenie with the Ottoman Order of Chastity, third class.

Ancien
Serai de l'Aga des
Janissaires

djamissi

Balikbazari Kapoussi
(Porte du Marché aux Po...
Douane

Baghdjé

Porte du

djamissi

Mosquée de la
Sultane Walide

Souleimanié kalaa

Koeschk

Tombeau d'Ab

Khan

Humamdjiler Kha

Harem

Khan de Waride

Bain
VIEUX
SERAI

Tschalakhane
djamissi

Tschenebel Hamam

Vau Khan

Mosqué de Mohammed pascha

Merdjan djam

Mosquée du
S. Osman

BESESTAN

Wezir khan   Wezir Se

Mosquée de
S. Bayezid II

Mosq. d'Ali pascha

Mosquée
Ecole

Tombeau de
Bayezid

Palais prétendu
de Belisaire

AY

Abattoir

Ecole

Citernede des
Colonnes

Merdjan Aga djamissi

Baghrakhan

Atmeidan
Hippodrome

M

CONDOSKALE

Mohammed Pascha
djam

Timarkhan

Horchun Pascha djam

Agiakiriake Eglise

Mosquée
Panagiatis elpidos

Serai de la Sult. Esma

Koutschouk Aya So

Tabarets

Kadrigha limani

Béghlik Serai

Koum Kapou

Tschatladi Kap

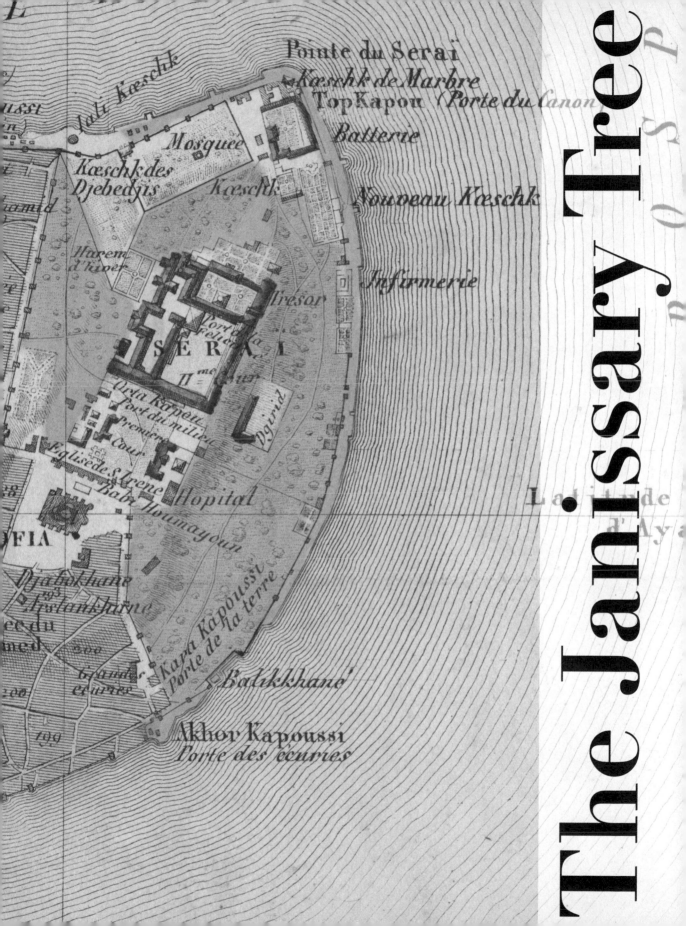

The Janissary Tree

Set in Istanbul in 1836, The Janissary Tree was the first Yashim mystery to be translated into over forty languages. The story revolves around the Ottomans' notorious infantry corps, the Janissaries, who were also craftsmen, musicians and fine chefs. When they mutinied, they would overturn the huge cauldrons in which they cooked their rice, and drum on them with wooden spoons.

" 'The other day you quoted something to me – an army marches on its stomach. Who said that? Napoleon?'

Palewski pulled a face. 'Typical Napoleon. In the end his armies marched on their frozen feet.'

'But you remember how the Janissaries named their ranks?'

'Of course – by kitchen duties. The colonel was called the soup cook. Sergeant-majors carried a long wooden ladle, and for the men, losing a regimental kettle in battle was the ultimate disgrace.'

“ Yashim found the Polish ambassador in a silken dressing gown embroidered with lions and horses in tarnished gold thread, which Yashim supposed was Chinese. He was drinking tea and staring quietly at a boiled egg, but when Yashim came in he put up a hand to shield his eyes, turning his head this way and that like an anxious tortoise. The sunshine picked out motes of dust climbing slowly toward the long windows.

'Do you know what time it is?' Palewski said thickly. 'Have tea.'

'Are you ill?'

'Ill? No. But suffering. Why couldn't it be raining?'

Unable to think of an answer, Yashim curled up in an armchair and let Palewski pour him a cup with a shaking hand.

'Meze,' Yashim said. He glanced up. 'Meze. Little snacks before the main dish.'

'Must we talk about food?'

'Meze are a way of calling people's attention to the excellence of the feast to come. A lot of effort goes into their preparation. Or, I should say, their selection. Sometimes the best mezes are the simplest things. Fresh cucumbers from Karaman, sardines from Ortaköy, battered at most, and grilled . . . Everything at its peak, in its season: timing, you could say, is everything.'

Palewski, hung over, offers Yashim a cup of tea

CIGAR PASTRIES WITH FETA
sigara böreği

Filo pastry – *yufka*, in Turkish – has been known to the Turks for centuries, and is still made across Anatolia by housewives wielding three-foot rolling pins, *oklava*. To replicate their effort would be a counsel of perfection: easier to use commercial filo pastry.

Simple to make, impressive, and utterly delicious, these cigar pastries are perfect Ottoman finger food, good for meze and parties. Just don't expect them to last long once they've been served.

- Crumble the feta into a bowl and mash it with a fork, then add the egg and the chopped herbs and mix well.
- Stack five sheets of filo on a board and slice them through to make ten five inch strips. Keep a damp tea towel handy to pop over the filo so it won't dry out.
- Lay a strip on the board, running away from you lengthways. Put a teaspoonful of mixture on the near end, and roll it up. Halfway along, turn in the sides to tuck the ends in. Roll it up until about an inch from the end of the sheet, which you should wet with a brush. That seals the filo and keeps it rolled.
- As you finish them, put the cigars in a dish under another damp tea towel.
- Heat the oil in a frying pan. When it's hot, fry half the cigars for about five minutes, turning now and then to brown them all over. Remove them to a dish covered in kitchen paper to drain the oil, and fry the other half.
- Eat them straight away. You can make different stuffings, with baked aubergine or some roasted pumpkin mashed with feta and dill, for instance, or spicy lamb mince.

feta cheese 200g/8oz
egg 1
parsley, mint and dill a big bunch, chopped fine
filo pastry 5 sheets
olive oil 3tbsp

The Janissary Tree

" At the head of the stairs Palewski paused to catch his breath and analyze the peculiar mixture of fragrances seeping through the lighted crack at the foot of the door in front of him.

Yashim the Eunuch and Ambassador Palewski were unlikely friends, but they were firm ones. 'We are two halves, who together become whole, you and I,' Palewski had once declared, after soaking up more vodka than would have been good for him were it not for the fact, which he sternly upheld, that only the bitter herb it contained could keep him sane and alive. 'I am an ambassador without a country and you—a man without testicles.'

Yashim had considered this remark, before pointing out that Palewski might, at a pinch, get his country back; but the Polish ambassador had waved him away with a loud outbreak of sobs. 'About as likely as you growing balls, I'm afraid. Never. Never. The bastards!' Soon after that he had fallen asleep, and Yashim had employed a porter to carry him home on his back.

Something else he found it hard to identify, pungent and fruity

The impoverished diplomat sniffed the air and adopted a look of cunning sweetness that was entirely for his own benefit. The first of the smells was onion; also chicken, that he could tell. He recognized the dark aroma of cinnamon, but there was something else he found it hard to identify, pungent and fruity. He sniffed again, screwing his eyes shut.

Without further hesitation or ceremony he wrenched open the door and bounded into the room.

'Yashim! Yashim! You raise our souls from the gates of hell! Acem Yahnisi, if I'm not mistaken—so like the Persian *fesenjan*. Chicken, walnuts, and the juice of the pomegranate!' he declared.

Yashim, who had not heard him come up, turned in astonishment.

Palewski saw his face fall.

'Come, come, young man, I ate this dish before you were weaned. Tonight, let us give it in all sincerity a new and appropriate name: The ambassador was out of humour, and now is delighted! How's that?'

CHICKEN WITH WALNUT AND POMEGRANATE
acem yahnisi

This is the first recipe Yashim cooks in *The Janissary Tree*, and his friend Palewski guesses what it is by sniffing. You can also make it with duck, or pheasant, after which it is named in Persian *Fesenjan*.

- Toast the walnuts in a dry frying pan over a fairly hot hob. Stir them until they catch, then cool them down and grind them fairly fine in a blender or pound in a mortar.
- Melt half the butter and oil together, and brown the chicken with a pinch of salt. Remove to a plate.
- Put the rest of the oil and butter in the pan, lower the heat, and fry the onions to translucency: if they brown a little, so much the better. Return the chicken and cover with the stock (or water). Bring to a boil, then lower the heat again and simmer, covered, for 30 minutes.
- Add pomegranate molasses, ground walnuts, sugar and all the spices. Replace the cover and simmer for an hour, with the occasional stir to stop the walnuts sticking to the bottom.
- Garnish with pomegranate seeds, and serve with a fresh salad and rice.

walnut halves 250g/8oz
butter 50g/2oz
olive oil 3 tbsp
chicken thighs 1kg/2lb, *skinned*
onions, chopped 2
pomegranate molasses 5 tbsp
chicken stock 500ml/1 pint *(see p52)*
sugar 2 tbsp
turmeric 1 tsp
cinnamon ½ tsp
ground nutmeg ½ tsp
ground black pepper ½ tsp
salt
seeds from a pomegranate

Pomegranate Molasses
nar ekşisi

You can make molasses from most fruit juice – apples, grapes and berries, too. A ratio of four cups juice to a cup of sugar, with the juice of a lemon, makes a little over a cup of molasses.

fresh pomegranate juice
1l/2pints
sugar 200g/1 cup
juice of a lemon

- Stir the ingredients together in a heavy-bottomed pan, constantly and tirelessly, on a medium high heat, for up to an hour until it reduces to a syrup. It's not so much a recipe as an activity; just don't let it catch and burn.
- Bottled, it will keep for a few weeks in the fridge. Fruit syrups make delicious drinks, mixed with water. You can even make a syrup of red poppies, soaked in water – but you must snip off the black centres of the petals first!

PLAIN RICE
pilav

Yashim uses long grain white basmati and cooks it Persian style, to produce a dry, fluffy rice with a delicious golden crust. The Ottomans used a lot of butter in their cooking, where modern Turks might use olive oil. Clarified butter, the Indian ghee, comes in a tin. It keeps well and is available in ethnic groceries.

- Soak the rice in warm water for half an hour, and wash it until the water runs clear.
- Put the pan on a high heat, cover the rice with boiling water from the kettle, add a pinch of salt, and boil for about eight minutes until the water (or stock) has been absorbed and lunar craters appear on the surface. Check for doneness: grains should have a distinct bite. Add a splash more boiling water if you need to.
- In a second pan on a low heat, melt a tablespoonful of butter. Gently transfer the rice into this pan, scattering the grains over the butter. Lay a clean tea towel over the top, clap on the lid, and steam on a very low heat for ten minutes or so.

basmati rice 500g/1lb
salt
butter or ghee 2 tbsp

The rice will be fluffy, the grains separate, and everyone will fight to eat the golden crust at the bottom of the pan.

A Spring Pilaf
taze fasulyeli pilav

When the first small broad beans appear in Spring, nothing could better this simple pilaf with dill.

- Soak the rice in warm water for half an hour, and wash it until the water runs clear.
- Pod the beans, if fresh, sweat them in a generous dollop (1 tbsp) of butter for a minute or two, then add a splash of water and a pinch of salt and let them steam for a few minutes longer, until tender. Ideally you should remove the skins, but you needn't bother unless they are old and tough, or you have the Validé herself, the sultan's mother, coming to dinner. Set them aside.
- Drain the uncooked rice. Melt the rest of the butter in a heavy pan, and stir in the rice over a low heat. After a few minutes, when the grains begin to stick, add salt and pour stock or water over the rice to barely cover.
- Simmer gently until the liquid has all but disappeared. If you test the rice, it will still be nutty.
- Gently stir the beans and half the chopped dill into the rice, and cover the pan with a cloth and a lid. Over a whisper of heat, let the rice steam for fifteen minutes. Sprinkle the rest of the dill on top, take the pan off the heat and let it stand in a warm place, covered, until you are ready to eat it.
- Turn the rice out into a dish, helping to fluff it out with a fork.

basmati rice 500g/1lb
broad beans 300g/10oz fresh or 200g/½lb frozen
stock or water
fresh dill a handful, chopped
butter 2 tbsp
salt ½ tsp

Yashim struck a Lucifer and lit the lamp, trimming the wick until the light burned steadily and bright. It fell on a neat arrangement of stove, high table and a row of very sharp-looking knives, suspended in mid air by a splice of wood.

There was a basket in the corner and from it Yashim selected several small, firm onions. He peeled and sliced them on the block, first one way and then the other, while he set a pot on the stove and slipped enough olive oil into it to brown the onions. When they were turning, he tossed in a couple of handfuls of rice which he drew from an earthenware crock.

Long ago he'd discovered what it was to cook. It was at about the same time that he'd grown disgusted with his own efforts to achieve a cruder sensual gratification, and resigned himself to more stylised pleasures. It was not that, until then, he had always considered cooking as a woman's work: for cooks in the empire could be of either sex. But he had thought of it, perhaps, as a task for the poor.

Long ago he'd discovered what it was to cook

The rice had gone clear, so he threw in a handful of currants and another of pine nuts, a lump of sugar and a big pinch of salt. He took down a jar from the shelf and helped himself to a spoonful of oily tomato paste which he mixed into a tea glass of water. He drained the glass into the rice, with a hiss and a plume of steam. He added a pinch of dried mint and ground some pepper into the pot and stirred the rice, then clamped on a lid and moved the pot to the back of the stove.

He had bought the mussels cleaned, the big three inch mussels which grew on the Galata bridge, so all he had to do was to slide a flat blade between the shells and prise them open on their hinges, dropping them into a basin of water. The rice was half-cooked. He chopped dill, very fine, stirred it into the mixture and tipped it out onto a platter to cool. He drained the mussels, and stuffed them, using a spoon, closing the shells before he laid them head to toe in layers in a pan. He weighted them down with a plate, added some hot water from the kettle, put on a lid and slid the pan over the coals.

FOR STUFFED MUSSELS, SEE NEXT PAGE

RAM'S FRIES
koç yumurtası

Not easy to find these days, but it would be a shame not to offer a recipe for testicles.

- Chop the parsley fine and mix with lemon juice and a splash of oil.
- Slice the testicles in half. Dust them in flour seasoned with a pinch of salt and a pinch of isot biber (see page 14), dip into the beaten egg and brown in the hot oil.
- Drizzle with the parsley sauce and serve.

parsley a bunch
juice of a lemon
olive oil
ram's testicles, or fries 12
plain flour 1 tbsp
salt
pepper
isot biber
an egg, beaten

The same method suits herring roes, which are more easily sourced.

STUFFED MUSSELS
midye dolması

One of the slowly disappearing sights of Istanbul is the mussel man, with his tray of gleaming great mussels stuffed with rice and currants. In Yashim's day there were many wandering snack merchants, right down to men who sold offal on sticks, which people would buy to feed to the street dogs. That was a meritorious act, as is stuffing your own mussels and serving them cool to your friends.

- In a frying pan melt oil and butter, and soften the onion with the pine nuts.
- Stir in the rice and cook for three minutes. Stir in the tomato, and as it starts to soften add the currants, sugar, salt, pepper and spices, with a squeeze of lemon and boiling water to drench the rice, but not quite cover it. Clap on the lid and simmer until the liquid is absorbed and the rice *al dente* – a few minutes at most. Give it a stir, taste for seasoning –more heat? More lemon? Salt? – and set aside to cool.
- Clean the mussels, removing beards and discarding any that will not close when given a sharp rap on the side of the sink. As they are done, drop them into a bowl of warm salty water, to encourage them to open.
- Slide a knife between the jaws of each mussel, close to the hinge, and run it around, taking care not to break the shells apart completely. With a little flip, lay them out flat on their backs in a pan to catch any liquid. The best tool for the job is an old-fashioned, flat-bladed table knife, the sort with a bone handle – firm and slim enough to persuade the shell open, not sharp enough to cut you when you slip.

olive oil 1 tbsp

butter 1tsp

large onions 2, chopped fine

pine nuts 2 tbsp

long grain rice 150g/5oz

tomato 1, peeled and chopped

currants 1 tbsp

sugar 1 tsp

salt

pepper

fresh chilli 1, chopped, or pul biber 1 tsp (see page 14)

cinnamon pinch

allspice pinch

nutmeg pinch

turmeric ½ tsp

lemon juice 2 tbsp

mussels 25 large

- Loosely fill the half-shells with your fingers, or a spoon, and close the mussels: a swipe with your thumb may help to seal them. Stack them in layers in a shallow saucepan. Add any remaining liquid, or a splash of water, pop a plate directly on top of the mussels to keep them firmly in place, and cover the pan. Simmer for fifteen minutes. If the pan gets too dry, add a little hot water.

- Take the mussels off the heat. Real pros will give them a lick of oil to make their coats shine. Serve cool, with lemons – unless you'd prefer them hot.

The Janissary Tree

FIERY EGGS AND PEPPERS
menemen

With an egg or two slipped on top, *menemen* is a dish that sustains truckers and sailors across Turkey, somewhere between breakfast and a snack lunch. It concentrates all that's simple, delicious and colourful about the eastern Mediterranean. Without eggs, the peppery dish makes a good hot accompaniment to rice and meat, or can be eaten cold as a meze.

- On a medium heat, set the onion to melt in the olive oil. When it becomes translucent, add the garlic. Stir it around for a few moments and then add the peppers, with the chilli or kırmızı biber. Let the peppers soften before adding the tomatoes and sugar.
- Cook for another ten minutes or so to reduce the liquid, sprinkle with salt and pepper, and make four hollows in the sauce with the back of a spoon.
- Crack an egg over each hollow – it doesn't matter if the whites run, as they will. Cover the pan and cook for a couple of minutes, until the whites are set.

olive oil 2 tbsp
onion 1, *halved and sliced*
garlic cloves 2, *crushed*
peppers 2, *red, yellow or green, sliced lengthways*
fresh red chilli 1, *sliced, or*
kırmızı biber 1 tsp
tomatoes 2, *peeled and chopped*
sugar ½ tsp
salt and pepper ½ tsp each
eggs 4

Menemen is served with yoghurt garlic sauce (see page 200), a sprinkling of chopped parsley, and fresh toast at breakfast time. Try it with coriander seeds, too, scattered in the pan as it heats up and crushed with the back of a wooden spoon before the oil goes in.

Mustafa the Albanian sniffed suspiciously at the bowl of tripe. Lifting the horn spoon that hung around his neck as a symbol of his office, he dipped it into the bowl and turned the contents over. Tripe. Onions. Regularly shaped, faintly caramelised. He dug down to the bottom of the bowl and examined the spoon carefully in the light for any specks or impurities. Satisfied, he lifted the spoon to his lips and sucked noisily. Tripe soup. He smacked his lips, his immediate fears allayed. Whatever secrets this young apprentice held in the recesses of his heart he could definitely make the proper article on demand.

Two anxious pairs of eyes followed the spoon to the Guild Master's lips. They saw the soup go in. They heard the soup flow about Mustafa's palate. They watched anxiously as he held his hand close to his ear. And then they watched, delighted, as he nodded curtly. An apprenticeship redeemed. A new master soupier born.

'It is good. Keep an eye on the onions: never use them too large. The size of your fist is good, or smaller.' He brought up his own massive paw and curled the fingers. 'Too big!' He shook the fist and laughed. The apprentice tittered.

Impatience led to coriander and hell fire

They discussed arrangements for the apprentice's formal induction into the guild, his prospects, the extent of his savings and the likelihood of his finding an opening within the next few years. Mustafa knew that this was the most dangerous moment. Newly fledged soupiers always wanted to start right away, whatever the circumstances. It took patience and humility to carry on working for an old master while you waited for a shop to come free.

Patience, yes. Impatience led to coriander and hell fire. Mustafa tugged at his moustache and squinted at the young man. Did he have patience? As for himself, he thought, patience was his second skin. How could he have lived his life, and not acquired patience in positively redemptive quantities?

THE GUILD-MASTER'S TRIPE SOUP
işkembe çorbası

Tripe is an acquired taste. It is rude and lusty and off-colour, which is why we should not abandon it in an age of processed food. Just a few generations ago people were intensely interested in animal innards. Offal, bone and sinew gave them food to eat, musical instruments to play, and footballs to kick around.

Even in Yashim's time tripe was hardcore. The soup was sold in Istanbul as a hangover cure, which is why the tripe soup shops stay open all night and close before lunch. But the ingredients are cheap and the method is simple, so if you can't take it, nothing much is lost.

- Put the tripe, salt, four cloves of garlic, the juice of a lemon and a splash of olive oil in a pan. Add the salt. Cover with water and bring it to the boil. Lower the heat and simmer for four hours, skimming off any scum, until the tripe is tender. Add more water if necessary to keep the tripe submerged.
- Take out the tripe, reserving the cooking liquid, and let it cool. Cut it into 1-inch pieces.
- In another pan melt the butter, stir in the flour, and cook for a couple of minutes. Then, stirring continuously, gradually add the tripe liquid.
- Add the milk and the chopped tripe. Cover and simmer for 30 minutes.
- Serve piping hot with a topping of pul biber flakes and the remaining garlic, chopped and mixed with vinegar.

beef tripe 1kg/2lb, washed
garlic 6 cloves
juice of lemon 1
olive oil
salt 1 tsp
butter 50g/2oz
plain flour 50g/2oz
milk 200ml/¾ cup
red pepper flakes 2 tsp
white wine vinegar 2 tbsp

The Janissary Tree

> At the baths he wanted heat, and more heat. When his head seemed banded with flaming hoops he let the masseur pummel him like dough and then plunged himself into the icy water of the frigidarium.

Later on his way home he fell upon the vegetable market in a sort of frenzy: his old friend George, the Greek vendor who arranged his wares like weapons in an armoury, or jewels on a tray, actually stepped out from behind his stall to lay a heavy hand on Yashim's arm.

'Slow. Slow,' he said in his bass profundo. 'You puts in this basket like a Greek robbers, this, that, everything. Say to George, what you wants to cook.'

He prised the basket from Yashim's hands and stood there massive and barrel chested in his dirty tunic, hands on his hips, blocking Yashim's way.

Yashim lowered his head.

'Give me the basket, you Greek bastard,' he said.

George didn't move.

'The basket.'

'Hey.' George's voice was very soft. 'Hey.' Louder. He picked up some baby cabbages. 'You wants?'

Yashim shook his head.

'I understand,' George said. He turned his back on Yashim and began to unload all the vegetables from his basket. Over his shoulder he said: 'Go, buy some fish. I will give you a sauce. You kebabs the fish, some Spanish onion, peppers. You puts on the sauce. You puts him in the fire. You eats. Go.'

Yashim went. When he had the fish, he came back and George was crushing walnuts open with his hands and peeling cloves of garlic,

Yashim cooks fish

He laid the skewers over the dull emb

which he put together in a twist of paper.

'Now you, effendi, go home and cook. The pepper. The onion. No, I don't take money from crazy mans. Tomorrow you comes, you pays me double.'

When Yashim got home he laid the fish and vegetables on the block and sliced them with a thin knife. The onions were sharp and stung his eyes. He riddled up the stove and chucked in another handful of charcoal. When he had threaded the pieces onto skewers he smashed the walnuts and the garlic with the flat of a big knife and chopped, drawing together the ever-dwindling heap with the flat of his hand until the hash was so sticky he had to use the blade to scrape it off his skin. He anointed the fish with the sauce and let it lie while he washed his hands in the bowl his housekeeper set out for him every morning and afternoon.

He laid the skewers over the dull embers and drizzled them with a string of oil. When the oil hissed on the fire he waved the smoke with a cloth and turned the skewers, mechanically.

Shortly before the fish was ready to flake from the stick he sliced a loaf of white bread and laid it on a plate with a small bowl of oil, some sesame seeds and a few olives. He stuffed a tiny enamelled tea-pot with sprigs of mint, a piece of white sugar and a pinch of Chinese tea leaves rolled like gunshot, poured in water from the ewer and crunched it down into the charcoal until its base bit into the glow.

Finally he ate, sitting in the alcove, wiping the peppers and the fish from the skewer with a round of bread.

Only then did he pick up the small folded note that had been waiting for him when he got home.

and drizzled them with a string of oil

FISH POACHED IN PAPER
kağıtta balık buğulaması

I don't buy fish at supermarkets; it can be as much as two weeks old. But their competition means that if you do have the luxury of a local fishmonger, he will probably be very good. In Istanbul markets the fish are displayed with their gills turned out, frilly and red like a houri's petticoats, so that the question of freshness can be decided at a glance. There may or may not be crushed ice: these fish won't hang about.

In the meantime there's a lot to be said for cooking with paper and string, *in cartoccio*. Your little parcels will seal in flavour and they look incredibly enticing on a plate. The surprise is that the parcels aren't baked, but poached.

- Cut the fish into 2 inch pieces. Cut some baking parchment into 6-inch squares, counting two squares to each piece of fish.
- Dampen the paper by flicking it with water from your fingers, and brush with olive oil.
- Lay two sheets of paper one above the other, at an angle, to form an eight-pointed star. In the middle set a piece of fish with some slices of fennel and onion, a sprinkle of parsley and a knob of butter. Salt and pepper to taste.
- Gather the points of the parcel together at the top and secure them with a loop of string tied in a bow.
- Carry on making parcels until all the fish is used up.
- Bring an inch of water to the boil in a shallow pan wide enough to hold all the parcels together. When it is boiling, lower the parcels into the water and cook for fifteen minutes.
- Serve *in cartoccio*, with lemon wedges.

boneless fillets of fish 4
olive oil
butter 4 tsp
fennel bulb 1, *finely sliced*
red onion 1, *finely sliced*
parsley small bunch, chopped
lemon 1
salt
pepper
string or good thread

" The provisioning of a great city, the kadi liked to remark, is the mark of a successful civilisation. In Istanbul it was a business that had been honed close to perfection by almost two thousand years' experience, and it could truly be said of the markets of Istanbul that there was not a flower, a fruit, a type of meat or fish that did not make its appearance there in season.

An imperial city has an imperial appetite, and for centuries the city had commanded daily tribute from an enormous hinterland. Where the Byzantines had managed their market gardens on the approaches from Thrace and Asia Minor, the turks, too, raised vegetables. From two seas – the warm Mediterranean and the dark, gelid waters of the Black Sea – it was supplied abundantly with fish, while the sweetest trout from the lakes of Macedonia were carried to the city in tanks. From the mountains of Bulgaria came many kinds of honey to be turned into sweets by the master sweet-makers of Istanbul.

It was a finely regulated business, all in all, from the Balkan grazing grounds to the market stall, in a constant slither of orders, inspections, purchases and requisitions. Like any activity that needs unremitting oversight, it was open to abuse.

An imperial city has an imperial appetite

The kadi of the Kerkoporta market had taken up his job twenty years before, and earned himself a reputation for severity. A butcher who used false weights was hanged at the doorway of his own shop. A greengrocer who lied about the provenance of his fruit had his hands struck off. Others, who had jibbed a customer, perhaps, or slipped out of the official channels to procure bargain stock, found themselves forced to wear a wide wooden collar for a few weeks, or to pay a stiff fine, or to be nailed by the ear to the door of their own shop. The Kerkoporta market had become a byword for honest dealing, and the kadi supposed that he was doing everything for the best.

The merchants found him officious, but they were divided as to the best way to deal with him. A minority were for clubbing together to manufacture some complaint against him from which he would be unlikely to recover; but the majority shrugged their shoulders and counselled patience. The kadi, some suggested, was merely establishing his price. Will not an ambitious carpet dealer wax lyrical over the colours and qualities and rarity of his carpet, as a prelude to negotiation? Will not a young wrestler hurl all his strength into the contest, while the older man uses no more than he actually needs to use? The time would come, they argued, when the kadi would start to crack.

BAKED LAMB STEAKS
Konya kebabı

No garlic? No butter, or oil? No spices? I first came across this recipe in a little book of Turkish cookery written by the gloriously named Venice Lamb, put out by my English publisher, Faber, in the late 1960s. Weird, even primitive, it tastes very good, and is a speciality of Konya, the seat of the Seljuks, a pre-Ottoman Turkish dynasty who ruled over much of Anatolia in the declining years of the Byzantine Empire. It's also the birthplace of the Mevlevi sect of Whirling Dervishes. Yashim, who travelled widely in the Ottoman Empire and beyond, would have cooked this in Istanbul, where it is known as *kuzu kapama* and traditionally heralds the coming of spring.

- Set the oven to a moderate heat, 170°C.
- Lay the steaks whole in an earthenware pot with a lid. Make up a paste with the flour and some water, and use it to cement the lid so that no steam escapes. Bake the lamb just as it is for two hours.
- To skin the tomatoes, cut a shallow cross on the bottom of each one and drop them into boiling water for a minute. The skin will slide away. Cut out the stalk root.
- Lift the lid of the pot, breaking the seal, and lay the spring onions, the lettuce and the tomatoes on top of the meat, with the herbs and a generous pinch of salt and sprinkling of black pepper.
- Replace the lid, without re-sealing, and bake for half an hour.

lamb steaks 1kg/2lb
plain flour 2 tbsp
large tomatoes 3
spring onions 250g/8oz, *trimmed and split lengthways*
cos lettuce 1, *split in two*
mint and parsley sprigs
salt
pepper

KEBAB OF PILGRIM OSMAN
Hacı Osman kebabı

A related dish comes from the first Ottoman cookbook to be published in English. The recipes in Turabi Efendi's *A Turkish Cookery Book* (1864) were mostly from Mehmet Kamil's *Melceü't Tabbahin, A Chef's Refuge*, published twenty years earlier.

Perhaps Osman, who had completed his pilgrimage to Mecca, deserved a treat? The Janissaries, on the other hand, ate meat every day. Palace records show that the imperial kitchens cooked 35,000 sheep (and over 50,000 hens) in the year 1574: more sheep than, say, aubergines (27,190).

- Cut the lamb into pieces 'the size of a walnut', or about 2 inches square, and rinse them in water.
- Put them into an earthenware pot, along with the onion, salt, pepper, and cinnamon, well mixed.
- Seal the lid with flour paste (see p44) and bake in a moderate oven at 170°C for three hours.

lamb 1kg/2lb
onions 2, *chopped*
salt
pepper
ground cinnamon 1 tsp

PILAF WITH CHICKPEAS
nohutlu pilav

Mehmet the Conqueror's Grand Vizier used to serve this as a working lunch in *divan*, the cabinet meeting held on a Friday. Into it he tossed a gold chickpea for some lucky pasha to discover (or break a tooth on): the Ottoman version of a sixpence in the Christmas pudding, perhaps. The sultan did not attend divan in person, but he might watch and listen from a small curtained window overhead. Or he might not: his pashas never knew.

- Soak the rice in warm water for half an hour, and wash it until the water runs clear.
- Melt the onions in butter. When they are soft, add the chickpeas.
- Stir the rice into the pan. After a couple of minutes add a pinch of salt and enough stock or water to cover the rice and a little more. Turn up the heat and check the rice when all the stock has been absorbed; it should be a little nutty. If necessary add a little more stock and continue cooking until the rice is almost done.
- Cover the pan with a cloth and a lid. Over a whisper of heat, or none, let the rice steam for fifteen minutes.
- Turn the rice out into a dish, helping to fluff it out with a fork.

basmati rice 500g/1lb
onion 1, finely chopped
butter or ghee 1 tbsp
chickpeas 250g/8oz, soaked overnight and boiled tender (tinned chickpeas are handy, too)
salt ½ tsp
stock or water

The Janissary Tree

CORIANDER CHICKEN WITH LEMON AND SUMAC
kişnişli ve limonlu tavuk

The Ottomans loved using coriander, with its pungent fresh leaves and silky, warming seeds, but when the empire was abolished in 1923 it seemingly fell from grace and coriander leaves barely feature in modern Turkish cookery. It goes well with the tart bite of lemon and sumac.

- Crush and chop the garlic in the salt. Roughly chop the coriander leaves, and mix them both in a large bowl with the garlic, lemon juice, pul biber, cumin, and salt. Stir the marinade through the chicken pieces and set aside for six to eight hours, preferably in the fridge, turning the chicken now and then.
- Melt the ghee or butter in a baking dish in a hot oven (220C). When it is hot, pour in the chicken with its marinade, stir to baste the meat with the fat, and return to the oven for thirty minutes, or until the chicken is cooked through.
- Sprinkle with the lemony sumac, and serve with pide and salad, or a plain pilaf.

garlic *2 cloves*
coriander *large bunch*
lemon *juice of 2*
pul biber *1 tsp*
cumin *1 tsp*
salt *1 tsp*
chicken pieces *(thigh or breast) skinned 1 kg/2lb*
OR
whole chicken, *jointed and skinned 1½ kg/3lb*
ghee or butter *3 tbsp*
sumac *1 tsp*

George the Greek came swarming out from behind his stall as Yashim stood picking over the remains of a basket of salad leaves. The sight seemed to drive him into a frenzy.

'What for yous comes so late in the day, eh? Buying this old shit! Yous an old lady? Yous keeping rabbits now? I puts everything away.'

He set his hands on his hips.

'What you wants, anyways?'

Yashim tried to think. If Palewski came to dinner, as promised, he'd want something reasonably substantial. Soup, then, and manti – the manti woman would have some left, he was sure. He could make a sauce with olives and peppers from the jar. Garlic he had.

'I'll take that,' he said, pointing out an orange pumpkin. 'Some leeks, if you have them. Small is better.'

'Some very small leeks, good. Yous making balkabagi? Yous needs a couple of onions, then. Good. For stock: one carrot, onion, parsley, bay. Is twenty five piastres.'

'Plus what I owe you from the other day.'

'I forgets the other days. This is today.'

> *He dropped the stock vegetables into a pot*

He found Yashim a string bag for his vegetables.

The manti woman was still at work, as Yashim had hoped. He bought a pound of meat and pumpkin manti, half a pint of sour cream in the dairy next door and two rounds of borek, still warm from the oven. And then, for what felt like the first time in days, he went home.

In his room he lit the lamps, kicked off his street shoes and hung his cloak on a peg. He trimmed the wicks and opened the window a fraction of an inch to clear the accumulated air. With an oil-soaked scrap of rag and a handful of dry twigs he started a fire in the grate and scattered a few lumps of charcoal on top. Then he started to cook.

He dropped the stock vegetables into a pot, added water from the jug, and settled it on the back of the stove to reach a simmer. He slid a ripple of olive oil over the base of a heavy pan and chopped onions, most of the leeks, and some garlic cloves, putting them on to sweat. Meanwhile with a sharp knife he scalped the pumpkin, scooped out the seeds and put them aside. Careful not to break the shell he scraped out the orange flesh with a spoon and turned it with the onions. He threw in a generous pinch of allspice and cinnamon, and a spoonful of clear honey. After a few minutes he set the pan aside and dragged the stockpot over the coals.

He put a towel and a bar of soap in the empty water basin and went downstairs to the stand-pipe in the tiny back yard, where he unwound his turban and stripped to the waist, shivering in the cold drizzle. With a gasp he ducked his head beneath the spout. When he had washed he towelled himself vigorously, ignoring his smarting skin, and filled the water jug. Upstairs he dried himself more carefully and put on a clean shirt.

Only then did he curl up on the divan and open the Validé's copy of Les Liaisons Dangereuses. He could hear the stock bubbling gently on

In his hand he carried a silken bow string, looped around his fist

the stove; once the lid jumped and a jet of fragrant steam scented the room with a short hiss. He read the same sentence over a dozen times, and closed his eyes.

When he opened them again he was not sure if he had been asleep; there was someone knocking on the door. With a guilty start he scrambled to his feet and flung back the door.

'Stanislaw!'

But it wasn't Stanislaw.

The man was younger. He was kicking off his shoes, and in his hand he carried a silken bow string, looped around his fist.

The Janissary Tree

STOCKS

Yashim always has a stock on the go. His meat stocks are made with bones and scraps, a bayleaf, a carrot sliced on the diagonal, an onion pricked with a clove or two and a stick of celery. If the stock boils it will become cloudy.

The earliest Turkish cookbook in English begins with a recipe for a large stock, *Et Suyu*, suitable for soup. I reproduce it here exactly as it is given, for flavour in every sense:

Meat stock

"Wash the meat well, and put it in a stew pan with salt, onions, celery and water. Then set the pan on the fire, when it starts boiling, skim it well, and let it simmer until the meat separates from the bones. Then pass the broth through a sieve."

4lb shin of beef or knuckle of veal
4 onions cut in four crosswise
1 stick celery
salt
4 quarts water

Vegetable stock

Gently fry chopped onion, garlic, carrot and some aromatic like celery or celeriac, a pepper chopped small, and herbs. Fry them until soft, then add water and a pinch of salt. Simmer for 30 minutes, then sieve, pressing the pieces against the mesh with a wooden spoon.

Chicken stock

Put a small fresh chicken in a pan, cover with cold water, and add 1tsp each of salt and peppercorns, a bayleaf, a peeled whole onion with a couple of cloves nailed into it, a carrot thickly sliced. Bring to a gentle simmer, taking care not to let it boil, and cook for half an hour, covered, on top of the stove. Take out the chicken, which will be good for other recipes, and discard the vegetables and bayleaf.

LADIES' THIGHS
kadınbudu köfte

This classic Ottoman palace dish is surprisingly quick and easy to make. The palace ladies were not skinny supermodels, either. I learned this recipe from the conductor Cem Mansur, who cooked it for me at his beautiful house in Ortakoy.

- Sweat the onion with olive oil until it begins to colour, then raise to a high heat and turn in half the minced lamb. When the lamb is browned and dry, mix in the cooked rice.
- Turn the mixture into a bowl, add the remaining raw lamb, and stir it up with a hefty pinch of salt, the ground cumin and thyme, parsley and some fresh pepper.
- When everything is well mixed together roll little meatballs, about the size of an apricot, between your hands. Make them slightly oval, and slightly flat.
- Roll in plain flour, dip in a bowl of beaten egg and fry them in sunflower oil at a high heat for 5 minutes on each side.

onion, *finely chopped 1*
olive oil, *1 tbsp*
minced lamb 450g/1lb
basmati rice, *cooked,*
a handful
salt
cumin, *ground 1 tsp*
dried thyme 1 tsp or **fresh**
thyme a sprig
parsley, *finely chopped, a bunch*
pepper
flour 2 tsp
egg, *beaten 1*
light sunflower or rapeseed oil

Yashim would serve them with a chickpea pilaf and a green salad, with a wedge of lemon. You should do the same – or make them really small and have them as meze, or snack, with drinks. Instantly you are in the seraglio....

PUMPKIN SOUP
balkabağı çorbası

Pumpkins have a rustic reputation belied by their appearance in this silky and sophisticated dish, which is happily very easy to rustle up. You could roast the pumpkin first, rubbed in oil and salt.

- Melt the butter in a saucepan and turn in the pumpkin and onion, stirring them for a few minutes on medium heat.
- Add the sugar, pour in enough stock to surround but not drown the pumpkin, bring to a gentle simmer and cook, covered, for 15 minutes until the pumpkin is soft.
- Mash the pumpkin with a potato masher or a blender and return to the pan. Add salt, pepper, and stock and bring it up to heat to simmer for a few minutes. Stir the soup and check the seasoning and consistency.
- Serve with a neat drizzle of yoghurt, and a sprinkling of parsley.

butter *75g/3oz*

pumpkin or squash *1kg/2lb, peeled, cut into 2cm/1" cubes*

onion *1, chopped*

sugar *1 tsp*

chicken stock *1litre/2 pints (see page 52)*

salt

pepper

yoghurt *150g/½ cup, slightly diluted*

parsley *small bunch, finely chopped*

" Murad Eslek walked back to the market. Now and then he had to flatten himself against the wall to allow other donkey carts to clatter by, but by the time he reached the square the first hubbub of the night had subsided. The vendors were busy with their arrangements of fruit and vegetables, vying against each other by building pyramids, amphitheaters, and acropolises of okra, eggplants, and waxy yellow potatoes, or of dates and apricots, in blocks and bands and fancy patterns of colour. Others, who had lit their braziers, were waiting for the coals to develop their white skin of ash, and using the time to nick chestnuts with a knife, or to load a thick skewer with slices of mutton. Soon, Eslek thought with a pang of hunger and anticipation, the meatballs would be simmering, the fish frying, the game and poultry roasting on the spits.

He, too, had another job to do before he could eat. Once he had checked with his vendors, and reckoned their bills, he took a tour of the perimeter of the market. He paid particular attention to dark corners, shadowed doorways, and the space beneath the stalls whose owners he did not serve.

Acropolises of okra, eggplants, and waxy yellow potatoes

He looked men in the face and recognized them quickly; now and then he lifted his head to scan the market as a whole, to see who was coming in and to watch for the arrival of any carts he didn't know.

From time to time he wondered what was keeping Yashim.

A troupe of jugglers and acrobats, six men and two women, took up a position near the cypress tree, squatting on their haunches, waiting for light and crowds. Between them they had set a big basket with a lid, and Murad Eslek spent a while watching them from the corner of the alley beneath the city walls until he had seen that the basket really did contain bats, balls, and other paraphernalia of their trade. Then he moved on, eyeing the other quacks and entertainers who had crowded in for the Friday market: the Kurdish storyteller in a patchwork coat; the Bulgarian fire-eater, bald as an egg; a number of bands—Balkan pipers, Anatolian string players; a pair of sinuous and silent Africans, carefully dotting a

blanket spread on the ground with charms and remedies; a row of gypsy silversmiths with tiny anvils and a supply of coins wrapped in pieces of soft leather, who were already at work snipping the coins and beating out tiny rings and bracelets.

He took another look across the market and thought of food, though he knew it would be a few minutes yet before he could eat. The air was already spiced with the fragrance of roasting herbs; he could hear the sizzle of hot fat dripping on the coals. He lifted a cube of salty white bread from a stall as he passed by and popped it in his mouth; then, since no one had rebuked him, he stopped a moment to admire the arrangement of the spit, worked by a little dog scampering gamely around inside a wooden wheel. Nearby he saw out of the corner of his eye a man flipping meatballs with a flat knife. He drew a few meatballs to the side of the pan, and Eslek stepped forward.

The Janissary Tree

Ottoman

Yeni Mahalle

Mosquée

Mosquée

HK TASCH

Mosquée

Palais de la

Mosquée de Sinan Pascha

Abord de Beschiktasch

Tscherlek de Moustafa Efendi

persan

chiktasch

C

Palais de la Sultane

ltane Begourn

N A L d

The Snake Stone

Serpenti di Petra in Italian, *Der Antiquar von Konstantinopel* in German, The Snake Stone deals with fallout from Greek independence in 1828 and takes us back into Istanbul's ancient past, before the Turkish conquest of 1453. There's talk of spice, and Byron's death, and dogs and doctors. And there is a lot of cooking.

An archaelogist comes for dinner

 'Dr Lefèvre, I welcome you to Istanbul.'

'The city ordained by Nature to be the capital of the world.' Lefèvre fixed his dark eyes on Yashim. 'She calls me like a siren, monsieur. I cannot resist her lure.' He drained his glass and set it down silently in the palm of his other hand. '*Je suis archeologiste.*'

Yashim brought out a tray on which he had set a selection of meze – a white bean piyaz with olives and tomatoes; some very small peppers stuffed with cheese and sliced, *beyaz peynir*; a selection of dwarf aubergines and courgettes, fried in a fragile batter. Palewski was brooding over his champagne. Lefèvre picked up a potato ball and popped it into his mouth.

'How shall I explain?' He began. 'To me, this city is like a woman.

What is Byzantium?

In the morning she is Byzantium. You know, I am sure, what is Byzantium? It is nothing, a Greek village. Byzance is young, artless, very simple. Does she know who she is? That she stands between Asia and Europe? Scarcely. Alexander came and went. But Byzance: she remembers nothing.'

His hand hovered above the tray.

Stuffed Chard
etli pazı dolması

This fashionable leafy vegetable was much loved by the Ottomans. In the garden it has all the virtues: beautiful to look at, with its thick, flat white (or red or yellow) stem and shiny green leaves, and more forgiving than spinach, which tends to bolt. Chard gives you two vegetables in one – the stems can be cooked like celery, the leaves like spinach; and it tastes good, too.

The Ottomans and their successors were and are very fond of things stuffed – *dolma*. Dolmabache, the late Ottoman palace on the shores of the Bosphorus, gets its name from the same root: it is built on land reclaimed by infilling. *Sarma* refers to things wrapped, usually in leaves – cabbage leaves, vine or fig leaves, though cherry and apricot leaves can be used, too. So the well-known Greek dolmades, rice wrapped in vine leaves, are actually sarma.

Here's how to do chard, Yashim style. Allspice and cinnamon, black pepper and maybe dried mint were traditional in dolma in Yashim's day.

- Make a stuffing by mixing in a bowl the minced meat with the onion and garlic, a generous handful of raw basmati rice, and all the seasoning you want – parsley, thyme, mint, coriander, cumin, allspice in any combination or quantity you like, and of course salt and black pepper. A chopped tomato if you want.
- Blanch the chard for thirty seconds in boiling water, rinse in cold water, and remove the very thickest part of the stalks from the leaves with a sharp knife.
- Put a leaf face down on a board, stem end towards you, and crush the stalk beneath the flat of your hand. You want the stalk limp and pliable. Lay a thumb-sized roll of stuffing on the leaf, a couple of inches from the edge. Fold the bottom over, fold the two sides in, and roll it up. Hold it tight until you've laid it in a shallow saucepan, seam down so it doesn't unravel.
- Make a dozen.
- Pour boiling water or stock over the rolls, to almost cover, and lay a plate on top, to keep them squeezed. Cover the pan, simmer for half an hour until most of the water has evaporated and the rice is cooked, and eat them dressed with some yoghurt beaten with garlic and mint. Or have them cold later on.

lamb or beef 250g/½lb, *minced*
onion 1, *grated*
garlic cloves 2, *finely chopped*
basmati rice, *a handful*
herbs, *chopped*
allspice ½ tsp, *ground*
cinnamon ½ tsp, *ground*
salt
pepper
chard 12 *large leaves*

ch Caracoulouchi, ou chef cuisinier des Janni.
suivre en grand costume.

You can do the same with cabbage leaves: separate them, boil for about five minutes in salted water, drain and refresh under the cold tap. Then use them just the same way. You could also try other leaves – runner beans, or fruit leaves like cherry or apricot.
You might replace the meat with a macedoine of vegetables – broad beans, carrot, tomato, pepper...

The Snake Stone

"Yashim stopped by the fish market on the Golden Horn. Still smarting from the Frenchman's indifference to the dishes he had so lovingly prepared he chose two lufer, the bluefish which all Istanbul took as the standard for excellence. He watched the fishmonger slit their bellies and remove the entrails with a twist of his thumb.

Yashim was proud of Istanbul – proud of its markets, the cornucopia of perfect fruits and vegetables that poured into them every day, proud of the fat-tailed sheep from Thrace which sometimes came skittering and bleating through the narrow streets. What other city in the world could produce fish to match the freshness or the variety offered by the Bosphorus, a finny highway running straight through the heart of Istanbul? Why, at any season of the year you could practically walk to Uskudar on the torrent of fish which passed along the straits –

'Don't wash it,' he said quickly. A fish would begin to deteriorate from the moment it lost its slimy protective coat.

A finny highway

A BASS IN SALT
tuzda pişmiş levrek balığı

A fresh bass is a beautiful fish, and this is a very stylish way of cooking it whole. The thick white flakes, tinged with browns and pinks, are mouth-wateringly juicy and the whole affair is somehow sultanic in splendour.

You want a whole fish, with its head and tail, gutted but not scaled – the fresher the fish, the more scales it will retain. If they slide off en masse beneath your fingers, it is not fresh enough.

- Find a baking dish big enough to hold it, and set the oven to 190°C.
- Line the bottom of the baking dish with ½ inch of salt, and lay the bass on it.
- Build a mound of salt over the fish, patting it all down neatly.
- Bake it in the oven for an hour. The salt will have formed a hard crust, which you can break dramatically at the table. Pry off the crust and the upper layer of skin – still armoured by its scales – and flip it away.
- Serve fillets from that side, with a bit of lemon and a scrunch of black pepper, then peel away the backbone and start in on the underside.

fresh bass, *whole, about 1kg/2lb*
coarse salt *1kg/2lb*
lemon *1*
black pepper

It needs nothing else – a salad, perhaps. And on the Ottoman table is always bread.

"Widow Matalya's brow furrowed and uncreased as she made her count. She champed her toothless gums together and the hairs trembled on a large black mole on her cheek. Now and again her fingers twitched. Widow Matalya did not mind, because she was asleep.

Widow Matalya dreams about chickens

She dreamed, as usual, about chickens. There were forty of them, leghorns and bantams, scratching about in the dust of the Anatolian village where she had been born more than seventy years ago, and the chickens in her dream were exactly the same as the chickens she had tended as a young woman, when Sipahi Matalya had ridden through her yard and sent them all squawking and flapping onto the roof of their own coop. Sipahi Matalya had taken her to Istanbul, of course, because he was only a summer sipahi, and they

She dreamed, as usual, about chickens

had shared a very happy marriage until he died; but now that her children were grown she thought very often of those forty birds. Awake, she wondered who had eaten them. Asleep, she checked that they were all safe. It was good to be young again, with all that ahead of one.

Twenty nine. Thirty. She scattered a little more grain and watched them pecking in the dirt. Thirty one. Thirty two. Or had she gone wrong? The noise of the chicken's beaks hitting the earth was confusing her. Bam! Bam! Thirty two, thirty three.

The lips stopped moving. Widow Matalya's eyes opened. With a sigh she levered herself ponderously off the sofa, adjusted her headscarf, and went to the door.

'Who is it?'

'It is Yashim, Hanum,' a voice called. 'I have no water.'

Widow Matalya opened the door. 'This is because the spigot in the yard is blocked, Yashim efendi.'

WIDOW MATALYA'S CHICKEN SOUP
Matalya'nın terbiyeli tavuk çorbası

When Ferdinand expelled the Jews from Spain in 1492, Sultan Bayezid made them welcome in the Ottoman Empire, saying; 'What king is this, that impoverishes his kingdom to enrich mine?' Many Jews settled in Thessalonica and other port cities. They spoke Castilian Spanish, known as Ladino, well into the twentieth century.

This comforting and nourishing soup is a staple of Jewish mamas worldwide, and is known as *avgolomeno* in Greece.

- Put chicken, onion, carrots, bayleaf, peppercorns and salt, with the parsley stalks, in a pot. Cover with water and bring to a quiet simmer, skimming off the scum as it rises. Don't allow the pot to boil, to keep the stock clear.
- After an hour lift out the chicken to cool while you strain the stock into a clean saucepan. Boil the stock until it is reduced by about a third, to concentrate the flavour.
- Pick the meat off the chicken and shred it between your fingers. Return the stock to a simmer, add the chicken and melt the vermicelli in it.
- Beat the eggs and the juice of half the lemon together in a bowl. As you beat, pour in a ladleful of stock and keep beating. If you are nervous of your eggs curdling, add another ladleful, beat, and pour it back into the pot, eggs, juice and all, stirring the soup to diffuse the flavour.
- The vermicelli will be done, so serve the soup with a sprinkle of chopped parsley and the rest of the lemon within reach.

chicken *whole, skinned*

onion *1*

carrots *2, split*

bayleaf *1*

peppercorns *½ tsp*

salt *1 tsp*

vermicelli *50g/2oz*

eggs *2*

lemon *1*

parsley *bunch*

AUBERGINE PARCELS WITH CHICKEN
tavuklu islim kababı

The American name, eggplant, well describes the way Turks regard this vegetable: mother of vegetables, the *fons et origo* of all good cooking. Treat aubergines firmly: you have to impose on them a bit, otherwise they consume oil and can even taste bitter. Stuffed, sliced, mashed, stewed, fried: the cooks at Topkapi Palace devised many ways of cooking aubergines. They had more varieties to play with than the solemn, shiny purple sort we're used to. In Turkey, aubergines range from near black to pale lilac, and from zeppelin to baseball bat. Use a peeler or a very sharp knife to take strips off the skin lengthways all round the aubergine, like a striped humbug, and soak sliced aubergines in cold salty water for half an hour, and squeeze out the water afterwards.

- Mix the garlic, lemon juice and allspice and pour over the chicken for a couple of hours in a cool place.
- Stripe the aubergines and slice lengthways finely – you will need eight slices from each one - and soak in cold salty water. After half an hour squeeze out the water.
- Heat a quarter of an inch of oil in a frying pan. When it starts to smoke, fry the aubergine slices in batches until they are golden. Spread them on kitchen paper to drain.
- On a board, lay two slices one across the other in the shape of a cross, put a piece of raw chicken in the middle, and wrap it in the aubergine. Tuck each parcel seam-side down onto an oiled baking dish.
- Shake the remaining marinade over the parcels, and sprinkle them with the almonds. Cover with foil and bake in the oven at 190°C for 40 minutes.

garlic cloves *3, crushed and chopped*
lemons *2, juiced*
allspice *½ tsp, crushed*
chicken thighs *8, skinless, boneless, cut in two*
aubergine (eggplant) *4*
sunflower oil
almonds *2 tbsp, flaked, toasted*

You could serve them with lemon, or with a yoghurt sauce; bring salad and a plain pilaf to the table.

Slipping out of Istanbul by caïque

" Venice and Istanbul: the client, and the source. For centuries, the two cities were locked together in trade and war, jockeying for advantage in the eastern Mediterranean. Istanbul had many faces but one, like Venice's, was turned to the sea. Like Venice, too, the greatest thoroughfares of Istanbul were waterways; people were forever passing from the city to Uskudar, from Uskudar to Pera, and from Pera to the city again, across the Golden Horn. The famous gondolas of Venice were no more central to life in the lagoon than caïques to the people of Istanbul, and while the Venetian gondola had its champions, most people would have agreed that the caique was superior in point of elegance and speed. Even after dark, the caiques swarmed around the landing stages like water beetles.

'Forget the ship's boat,' Lefèvre said quietly. 'It's better that I leave from here, unnoticed. Galata is all eyes.'

They left Yashim's lodging after dark, moving quietly on foot through the deserted streets. Lefèvre shouldered the satchel which apparently

Istanbul had many faces but one, like Venice's, was turned to the sea

contained everything he possessed. The narrow streets of the Fener were silent and dark, but Yashim led his companion through them by instinct, now and again pausing to feel for a corner stone, or to put his hand gently on the other man's shoulder. Once, a big dog growled out of the darkness, but it wasn't until they reached the landing stage that they met with any other sign of life: the city could have been uninhabited.

Down by the stage, Pera twinkled out across the black water of the Golden Horn. Lamps bobbed gently on the stems of the caïques drawn up against the quay, where a handful of Greek boatmen sat among the coils of rope, the creels and nets, murmuring together and smoking pipes which glowed red in the dark. Lower down the Horn a few ships rode at anchor, with lanterns at their prows. The water slapped darkly against the pilings where the caïques were moored.

A boatman uncoiled himself with catlike ease and stepped forwards.

'The Ca d'Oro? I know the ship.'

LAMB'S LIVER ALBANIAN STYLE
Arnavut ciğeri

In Venice very thin slices of liver are stirred for a few moments into a pan of onions which have melted slowly in olive oil (see p117). From Albania, across the Adriatic, comes this snappier Ottoman version.

- Mix the flour with salt and the isot biber, or paprika if you can't get the Turkish flaked chilli, and toss it with the sliced lamb's liver, coating the meat. A paper bag is useful for this.
- Slice the whole onion finely, and spread it on a serving plate.
- Heat up some olive oil in a heavy pan. Gently fry the garlic with a teaspoonful of cumin seeds until the scent is irresistible. Then fry the liver quickly for a few minutes. Throw in the sumac and shake the pan.
- Scatter the liver onto the onion rings, and serve hot, or cold, with lemon wedges for squeezing.

plain flour 2 tbsp

salt ½ tsp

isot biber 2 tbsp

lamb's liver 450g/1lb, *sliced a pencil's width*

red onion 1 *large*

olive oil

garlic cloves 2, *chopped*

cumin seeds 1 tsp

sumac 1 tsp

lemon wedges

CHICKEN LIVERS WITH LEMON AND SUMAC
limonlu tavuk ciğeri

Made with organic chicken livers this is a quick, delicious lunch to eat with bread or rice.

- Stir fry the onion, garlic and lemon peel, the two chillis and cumin.
- When the onions soften, fry the livers in the soffrito until they are nicely browned, add the tomato paste and the chicken stock.
- Cover and cook gently for ten minutes. Sprinkle with sumac and serve with lemon wedges.

onion 1, *sliced*
garlic cloves 2, *smashed and chopped in a little salt*
strip of lemon peel
isot biber 1 tsp
pul biber ½ tsp
cumin seeds 1 tsp
chicken liver 250g/8oz
tomato paste 1 tsp
chicken stock 150ml/½ cup
sumac ½ tsp

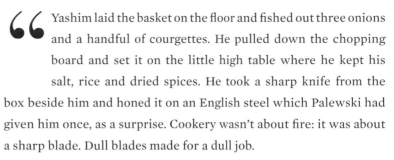

Yashim laid the basket on the floor and fished out three onions and a handful of courgettes. He pulled down the chopping board and set it on the little high table where he kept his salt, rice and dried spices. He took a sharp knife from the box beside him and honed it on an English steel which Palewski had given him once, as a surprise. Cookery wasn't about fire: it was about a sharp blade. Dull blades made for a dull job.

He ripped the outer skin from the onion using the blunt edge of the knife. He halved it and laid the halved pairs face down, curves touching. The knife rose and fell on its point. The board gave a momentary lurch and rocked to one side; Yashim continued chopping. He swept the slices to the edge of the board. The board rocked back again. Yashim raised one edge and swept his hand beneath it, dislodging a grain of rice.

For a few moments he stared at the tiny grain, frowning slightly.

Cookery wasn't about fire: it was about a sharp blade

Then he glanced up and poked his finger into the spaces between the rice crock and the salt cellar and the spice jars at the back of the table. A few grains of rice stuck to his fingers. He moved the crocks and jars to one side, and found several more.

Yashim rubbed the tips of his fingers together, opened the lid of the rice crock and looked inside. It was almost full, the little scoop buried in the grain to its hilt.

He looked around the room. Everything was in order, everything left as the widow would have left it after she'd been in to clean, the shawls folded, the clothes bags dangling on a row of hooks, the jug of water standing in the bowl.

But someone else had been in here.

Searching. Looking for something small enough to be hidden in a crock of rice.

Hazelnut and lemon pilaf
findıklı ve limonlu pilav

Master the essentials, and the pilaf world is open to you hereafter. This pilaf offers a delicious combination of earthy, crunchy hazelnuts with citrus backnotes, with a little extra zing – is it the chilli or the cumin?

Recipes can specify the volume of water for a certain weight of rice, but in the kitchen it depends on the size of your pan as well as the level of heat, and even the type of rice you use. My tip is to start with a little less water than you think you might need, and to add more from the kettle if necessary at the end of cooking. Do it a few times and you have a skill learned for life.

- Put the well-washed rice in a pan on the stove top, and cover with the same quantity of boiling water and the salt. Bring to the boil and cook for about ten minutes, until the rice is just done and all the water is absorbed. While the rice is boiling, melt half the butter with the oil in a frying pan over a low heat. Add the cumin and coriander, then the julienned lemon peel and chilli and the hazelnuts. Let them warm through but don't fry them.
- When the rice is done, tip it over the flavoured oil and butter mixture, stir gently, and return it all to the rice pan, giving it a stir to draw the flavours of spice and lemon through the rice. Dot the rice with the remaining butter, cover the pan with a cloth, and put the lid on firmly.
- Let the rice stand for at least ten minutes then fluff with a fork or wooden spoon.
- Scatter with the parsley and serve the pilaf with yoghurt sauce and lemon wedges.

basmati rice 250g/8oz, rinsed
salt 1 tsp
olive oil 1 tbsp
butter or ghee 1 tbsp
coriander seeds 1 tsp
cumin seeds ½ tsp
lemon peel, sliced into 3 'julienne' strips
fresh red chilli 1, sliced into thin strips, or *pul biber* 1 tsp
blanched hazelnuts 4 tbsp
parsley bunch, chopped

Try swapping the lemon peel for orange peel, the cumin for a pinch of saffron, the hazelnuts for almonds or pine nuts, or switch all three at once. At the warming stage you could toss in a handful of currants and chopped dried apricots. For a really warm winter glow cut a lid off a pumpkin, scoop out the seeds and rub the inside with a little oil and butter and salt. Put the pumpkin on a tray to bake in a moderate oven until it's slightly soft, maybe 45 minutes, then spoon it full of pilaf and return it to the oven for twenty minutes.

The Snake Stone

" Yashim settled into the bottom of a caique. The boatman shoved off with a flick of his long oar.

'Where to, efendi?'

'Fener Kapi,' Yashim said. The Fener landing stage. The boatman nodded: he was a Greek, and Greeks liked going to Fener.

For hundreds of years Fener had been the seat of the orthodox patriarchate, the soul of Greek Istanbul. In a city where many races and faiths mingled, the Patriarch was a link to the centuries before the Ottoman conquest, when Constantinople stood at the hub of the Christian world. For a thousand years, decked in the insignia of the Church, Byzantine emperors had born themselves proudly as God's anointed rulers on earth, greater than Popes or Patriarchs, wrapped in an unceasing round of prayer and ostentation - interrupted only by usurpation, betrayal, violent death, palace coups, murders, and the vicious political manoeuvring favoured by tyrants everywhere.

Worn steps led up to a battered door that had seen much since the last Emperor of Byzantium vanished in his purple buskins, as Ottoman troops swarmed across the walls of his desolate city. Behind that door lay the central piece in the elaborate mosaic of the Orthodox faith, which spread from the deserts of Mesopotamia and the roadsteads of the Aegean, to the mountains

The orthodox patriarchate, the soul of Greek Istanbul

of the Balkans and along the basalt cliffs of the Black Sea; all that was really left of the might and glory of the second Rome, the city of Constantine and Justinian; all that had survived the battle of iconoclasts and iconodules, the treachery of the Latins and the warlike prowess of the Turks.

Yashim gazed at the great door, then stepped along the street to a smaller gateway which for the last seventeen years had served as the main entrance to the Patriarchate. The great gate had been sealed as a mark of respect towards the Patriarch Bartholemew, hanged from its lintel by the sultan's order during the Greek riots of 1821.

At the gate, he asked for the Archemandrite.

Grigor was in his private office: a fat man with a big beard in a black surtout.

'Yashim – the angel!' Grigor opened his arms wide across a desk piled with packets and papers done up in purple ribbon.

The angel was Grigor's little joke; not one that Yashim particularly shared. As Grigor had once explained, Byzantine iconography represented angels as eunuchs. Angels stood on the threshold between men and God; eunuchs, between men – and women. Both were intermediaries, dedicated to serve.

The Snake Stone

GYPSY SALAD
çoban salatası

This is a Mediterranean salad concocted from ingredients easily lifted from other people's gardens. I could eat it forever, with a chunk of good bread.

- Peel the cucumber, halve lengthways, and scoop out the seeds with a spoon. Cut it into half-inch cubes. Cut and cube the pepper and tomato. Peel and slice the onion thinly from top to tail.
- Put everything into a salad bowl and crumble the feta on top, with the parsley. Combine the dressing ingredients in a small bowl, pour over the salad, toss and serve.

cucumber 1
red pepper 1
tomato 1
red onion 1
feta cheese 100g/4oz
parsley small bunch

Dressing
olive oil 4 tbsp
garlic ½ clove, crushed and chopped in salt
lemon juice 1 tbsp
sugar ½ tsp

BEAN SALAD
piyaz

The Ottomans adored picnics, which they often took at the Sweet Waters of Europe, up the Golden Horn. Put this together with good bread and a goat's cheese...

- Soak the beans overnight and boil them until they're tender. Drain, and mix them while still hot with the onion, garlic and oil in a salad bowl. Season with lemon juice, salt and sumac and stir in the parsley.
- Allow the beans to cool to room temperature – about an hour – and serve with lemons.

white beans 350g (a tin if you are in a rush)
red onion 1, finely sliced
garlic a clove, finely chopped
olive oil
juice of half a lemon
salt
sumac 1 tsp
parsley bunch, chopped
lemons

The Snake Stone

'*C'est bizarre*, Yashim. As he gets older, my son grows more and more infatuated by the European style – yet I, who was born to it, find that I prefer the comforts of oriental tradition. He hardly comes here any more, only to see me. His new palace delights him. I find it looks like a manufactory.'

Yashim inclined his head. The Validé was propped up on her sofa against a cloud of cushions, with the light as ever artfully arranged behind her head, a blind drawn across the little side-window, and a shawl across her legs. She walked rarely now, if at all; yet her figure was still graceful and the shadows on her face revealed the beauty she had once been and still, in a sense, remained. Her hands, a little lined, were white and delicate. Did the Validé not know that her son was dying at Besiktas?

'I am very old, Yashim, as you well know. Topkapi has been my home – some would say, my prison – for sixty years. It, too, is old. Well, the world has moved on from us both. By now, I like to think, we understand each other. We share memories. I intend to die here, Yashim, fully dressed. At the sultan's palace at Besiktas I'd be popped into a nightgown and tucked up in a French bed, and that would be an end of it.'

Yashim nodded. She was perfectly right. So many years had passed since a young woman, the captive of Algerian corsairs, had been delivered here, to the harem quarters of the aged sultan Abdul Hamit, that it was easy to forget how well the validé knew the European style. Aimée Dubucq du Riviery, a planter's daughter on the French

The Validé was propped up on her sofa against a cloud of cushions

island of Martinique: she was a Frenchwoman. The same inscrutable law of destiny that had taken her to the sultan's seraglio, where she had finally emerged as Validé, had led her childhood friend, little Rose, to the throne of France, as Josephine, Napoleon's own Empress.

A nightgown. A tight French bed. Yashim knew how the Europeans lived. Here, in the Empire, people divided their lives between what was public, and what was reserved for the family, between *selamlik* and *haremlik*: in the poorest homes, they were divided only by a curtain. But the Franks had a mania for divisions. They parcelled up their homes they way they segregated their actions. The Franks had special rooms for sleeping in, with fussy contraptions created for performing the act itself: all day long these bedrooms sat vacant and desolate, consoled by the dust rising in the sunlight – unless they belonged to an invalid. In which case the invalid herself shared the loneliness and desolation, far away from the activity of a household.

The Franks had dining rooms for dining in, and sitting rooms for sitting in, and drawing rooms for withdrawing into – as if their whole lives were not a series of withdrawals anyway, tiptoeing from one room and one function to the next, changing and dressing all over again, forever on the run from engagement with real life. Whereas in an Ottoman home – even here, in the harem – everyone was allowed to float on the currents of life as they sped by. If you were hungry, food was brought in. If you wished to sleep, you unfolded your legs, reclined, and twitched a shawl over yourself. If you were moody, someone was sure to drop in to cheer you up; ill, and someone noticed; tired, and nobody minded if you dozed.

YOGHURT
yoğurt

The word is Turkish, and it was brought west to the shores of the Mediterranean by the early nomadic Turks. It is easy to make, and each new pot is a sort of miracle.

full cream milk 1l/2 pints
live Greek yoghurt 1tbsp
runny honey 1 tbsp
salt

- Boil the milk for two minutes, stirring to prevent it rising out of the saucepan. Cool the pan in a bowl of cold water until you can comfortably dip a finger in the milk.
- Beat in the yoghurt and honey with a pinch of salt.
- Pour the milk into impeccably clean glass jars, or a bowl, and cover it: some people use a thermos flask. Keep the jars or bowl at room temperature overnight, because the yoghurt bacteria – including *lactobacillus bulgarius*, named after Bulgaria – needs warmth to do its work.
- In twelve hours that work is done and the yoghurt will have set. This first batch will be quite thin, but it will thicken slightly and improve in flavour over the next few days.

From now on use a tablespoon of your yoghurt to make a fresh batch: subsequent batches will become progressively thicker. If you like your yoghurt really thick, strain it in a colander or sieve lined with muslin or cheesecloth. The yoghurt lives in the fridge until you want to use it.

YOGHURT SOUP
yayla çorbası

'The Turks' main dish is soup,' wrote a German traveller in his diary for 1553, and this is one he might have encountered being prepared for the sultan and his household in the Topkapi kitchens. Varieties of this soup – with rice, wheat, or bulgar – still crop up all over Turkey, and beyond.

- Put the rice into a pan with the salted boiling water or stock and simmer for fifteen minutes until the rice is done. Other grains will take longer.
- Meanwhile, beat the yoghurt, flour and egg yolks together in a bowl. Dilute with a cup of cold water, beat again, and add it slowly to the rice.
- Stir the soup and simmer for five minutes. Add the mint and cook for another five minutes, then serve.

rice 200g/7oz (or barley or bulgar)
salt
water or stock 1l/2 pints
plain yoghurt 800ml/1½ pints
flour 2 tbsp
egg yolks 2
dried mint 2 tbsp

The Snake Stone

" The kebab shop was open to the street, where sliced hearts of lettuces were set out on a marble slab, besides sheep heads and feet, bowls of yoghurt and clotted cream, some *toorshan*, or pickles, and a small array of simple meze. A waiter was flicking away the flies with a clean cloth; he nodded at Yashim. Inside, china pots, plates and glasses sparkled on the shelves; a small fountain played in a corner. There was a glazed screen where a man with long moustaches ruled over a small empire of vases containing syrups and preserved fruits; on the other side the grills smoked against the wall, a half-tunnel of brick and clay lined with small coals. Various cuts of meat were on a spit; little skewers sizzled and popped above the flames; now

Little skewers sizzled and popped

and then the bare-armed cook slapped another *pide* on the hot bricks, and peeled it away as it began to crisp at the edges.

Yashim was led to a seat in the gallery, from where he could look down on the cooks. He saw the cook swing a pomegranate kebab from the coals and wipe the meat from the skewer onto a fresh pide. The lamb was cubed small: the best size. Yashim felt hungry: it wasn't every day you found a shop that offered such a succulent dish. He heard the cook speak: a Kurd, then, from the south. Which explained the pomegranate: the influence of Persia was strong in the south.

He and the waiter put their heads together and decided what Yashim would eat. As he sipped his *khoshab*, Yashim looked about him. It was a working crowd, he noticed: people who came to eat, not to loaf about with a pipe and a coffee...

Yashim's kebab arrived. He took a piece of smoking lamb between his fingers, and recognised its texture: this was good. He put it into his mouth, and with the same hand he broke off a piece of pide. He wondered that he had never eaten here before: he would like to come again.

The Snake Stone

AUBERGINE PURÉE
patlican salatası

A classic Ottoman meze, absolutely worth doing whenever you fire up a charcoal grill. Unlike the real thing, 'poor man's meat' is very forgiving on the grill, so you can start the aubergines off as soon as the coals get hot. The flame gives the finished purée an irresistible smoky taste. Don't forget the humble home fire, either. If you are burning wood in your fireplace, or maybe a woodburner, use it: an aubergine takes only a few minutes to cook.

- If you can rotate the aubergines over charcoal, so much the better: char the skins and pop the aubergines into a plastic bag when the flesh is pulpy. Otherwise, burn the skins on the gas or prick the aubergines with a fork, wrap them in foil and cook for at least half an hour in the hottest oven.
- Hold the aubergine by the stalk and peel away the skin. Scrape the flesh away with a spoon. Drop the flesh into a colander, and squeeze it gently to get rid of some of the water.
- Put the aubergines on a board and chop them to a pulp, while they continue to drain. Sweep them into a bowl, and mix in the garlic, the oil and the lemon juice. When they are well mixed, add the yoghurt, a pinch of salt and a twist of pepper and beat again. Check for seasoning.
- Serve the purée with a drizzle of olive oil and wedges of lemon, to eat on crusty bread.

aubergines (eggplant) 2
garlic 2 *cloves, crushed and chopped*
olive oil 2 *tbsps*
juice of 1 lemon
plain yoghurt 225g/8oz
salt
pepper
lemon wedges

Everything connects, of course, and given centuries of war and exchange between Russia and the Ottoman Empire it should come as no surprise that the Russians, substituting sautéed onion and tomato for the yoghurt, wisely adopted this as their 'poor man's caviar'. Versions of both are very popular across the Caucasus.

> Instead of taking a caique up the Golden Horn, Yashim descended the hill by the Sublime Porte and crossed in front of the Nurisyane, where he had found the litter-bearers the night before. Passing the entrance to the Egyptian bazaar he hesitated, then plunged in. The rich aromas of cinnamon and cloves, of cumin, coriander and pounded ginger made his head whirl. Mountains of vividly coloured powder rose on every stall, pungent spices gathered from all across the world, from the coasts of India and the mountains of China, from Persia and Arabia and the islands of the South Seas, brought here to this great entrepot of the world's trade by dhow, by carrack, by camel train and mule train, over deserts, through wild seas, crossing the passes of legendary mountain ranges, bartered and bought, fought for and pilfered, growing ever more valuable and rare until, at last, they reached this market on the edge of Europe, and vanished into a soup, or a dish of rice.

Yashim paused, dizzied by the reflection. What a world men had made! What adventures they undertook, simply to give colour and

Bartered and bought, fought for and pilfered

pungency to their diet! The bazaar was a treasure-house – yet nothing would be changed if a wind scattered the powders to the skies; no-one would starve; empires would not fall. The very stones of the bazaar would reek of spices a thousand years from now: what of it?

For something as trivial and evanescent, men could be killed. For an idea as immaterial as the scents which rose from the multicoloured hillocks of ground seeds, people were prepared to die.

The Snake Stone

BEETROOT SALAD
pancar salatası

Making a salad in summer is easy. Making something as good in winter is more interesting. This beetroot salad has a glorious colour and tastes lively and fresh.

- Wrap the beetroots in foil with a sprinkling of salt and half the cumin, and bake in the oven at 180°C for an hour, until they are tender to a fork.
- Let them cool and rub off the skins. Chop roughly into inch-sized pieces.
- Gently heat the pine nuts in a pan, until they start to colour. Toast the remaining cumin. Crumble the cumin seeds between your fingers into a bowl, with a glug of olive oil at the bottom.
- Add a pinch of salt, and toss the beetroot in the dressing with the yoghurt and the well-chopped white of leek. Scatter with pine nuts.

beetroots 3 *large or 4 small*
cumin seeds 2 *tsp*
pine nuts 2 *tbsp*
olive oil
salt
yoghurt 1 *tbsp*
white of a small leek, *finely chopped*

The Snake Stone

"The foresters had prepared the usual refreshments. A great black tent had been set up on the grass, with carpets and silver trays, and jugs of sherbet made of sour cherries and oranges covered with a little square of gauze, the edges weighted with dangling beads. To one side a fire was crackling under a tripod, on which a cook was preparing a bulgur pilaff, and a little further off two foresters were squatting by the tandir. Long before dawn they had begun to make and tend the fire, fetching brushwood and logs, reducing the wood to a pile of glowing coals. The pit they had dug was invisible beneath a covering of baked mud and sticks.

The cook had selected a lamb from the flock the day before. He had skinned and gutted the animal, studding its flesh with garlic spikes before he rubbed it with a mixture of yoghurt and sieved tomatoes, crushed onion and garlic, coriander and cumin. At dawn, when the fire began to sink, they trussed the lamb to a stake by its feet, and lowered it over the pit, setting the meat deeper and deeper as the morning progressed. Now the meat was cooking underground, sealed by a makeshift lid.

One of the foresters looked up. Recognising the naziry, he motioned to his companion, and the two men carefully raised the lid. The naziry saw the slightest trickle of smoke emerge from the pit. Overthrowing the lid, the forester bent forwards, and with a flash of his knife removed one of the kidneys, which he presented to the naziry on the

> *He rubbed it with a mixture of yoghurt and sieved tomatoes, crushed onion and garlic, coriander and cumin*

point. The naziry took the smoking morsel in his fingers and ate with relish, standing by the pit, gazing down into the glowing fire.

One of the foresters yawned. He was holding a green branch, which he waved gently over the roasting meat to chase the flies away.

The naziry settled himself on the carpet, crossing his legs beneath him, and watched the men draw the lamb out of the tandir. Beyond, the sunlight glittered on the surface of the bent; frogs croaked in the reeds;

swallows skimmed the water and rose twittering and whistling into the air. A servant picked up a silver tray and polished it carefully with a cloth. The cook nodded.

He arranged a mound of pilaff on the tray, then took the long knife hanging at his belt and began to carve the meat.

A horseman rode up the track and out of the trees. At the sight of the tent, and the smoking meat, he reined in and bowed from the saddle.

The sou naziry raised a hand, in greeting.

'May you eat well, efendi,' the stranger said, politely.

KLEPHTIC LAMB
kuzu çevirmesi

A whole lamb, rubbed with mountain herbs, spiked with garlic and cooked by lowering it slowly through the day into a fire pit, is something I like to imagine, read and even write about. In Turkey it is known as tandir kebab, and I know how it should taste – melting off the bone, slightly smoky, conjuring up memories of stepping on short meadow grass on a hot day, of scrambling over rocky scrub, and swimming in the Aegean. Best of all, the carcase is shaken over a dish to let the meat slip from the bone, with a stuffing made from currants, nuts, onions and herbs mixed with rice. The past masters at this were the klephts, Greek mountaineers and villagers who had turned bandit. The sheep was rustled, and the pit hid the smoke issuing from their mountain lairs. If you have space, and no need to hide the smoke, you can cook a whole or half lamb by a fire in about seven hours.

- Fix the beast to a stout cross-shaped frame, using strong wire. Hazel makes a good frame: mine is a steel clothes rail. Rig up some means of support, so that you can prop the lamb at an angle to face the fire.
- Get in a good supply of clean wood and build the fire an hour or two before you begin cooking.
- Prepare a briny marinade by mixing wine and water, salt, lemon juice, crushed garlic cloves, bruised chillis and herbs. The choice of aromatics is up to you. This is the basting liquor, with which you will repeatedly anoint the meat to prevent it drying out too fast. You can splash it on the meat from a jug using a rosemary twig, if you like, but a plastic bottle with a hole punched in the lid is also useful for squirting the basting juice upwards. Brush some of the liquor over the meat on all sides to begin with.
- When the fire is hot you should just be able to hold your

whole lamb
white wine a bottle
water 4l/8 pints
salt 500g/1lb
garlic 2 heads, peeled
olive oil
cumin seeds 1 tbsp
pul biber 1 tbsp
juice of two lemons
chilli 2
rosemary, oregano/marjoram,
mint, thyme bunches

The Snake Stone

hand to it, about two feet away, for ten seconds. This is just where you want your lamb to be over the next six hours. Lower the frame onto its support(s) and work it into position. Dig holes in the ground to anchor the feet of the frame if you need to. You are roasting at the fire, not over it, so don't lower the frame too far.

- Keep the fire reasonably lively throughout the process: as the logs burn and the embers build up the heat will increase, so you should need to feed it less as time goes on.

- Begin with the underside of the lamb, and turn it after a few hours, for another two hours, before finishing it off in its original position. Children, dogs and other men present are sure to take an interest in the entire process, for which wine and music are the natural accompaniments.

- A whole lamb feeds 30-40 people.

ROAST LAMB
fırında kuzu budu

Failing a fire pit, and shunning the barbecue as always too hot, or too slow, or just too darn small, I offer you this recipe for roast lamb. Leg is good, but shoulder is fattier and, cooked slowly, more succulent. Give yourself at least four hours to let the meat take on the marinade, and three to cook.

for the marinade
wine a medium glass
cumin seeds 1 tsp
pul biber 1 tsp
isot biber 1 tsp
zest of half a lemon
salt 1 tbsp
runny honey 1 tbsp

leg of lamb, 2½ kg/5 lb
a head of garlic, peeled
rosemary sprigs
olive oil

- Combine all the marinade ingredients in a bowl. Pour it over the lamb in its roasting tin and rub it in by hand. Let it marinade, covered, in the kitchen if it's not too hot, for anything up to 24 hours, but at least four.
- Set the oven medium hot, at 200°C/400°F/Gas 6. Peel and split most of the garlic cloves, and stud the meat with them slipped into holes you make with the point of your knife.
- Finally, baste the lamb with a generous splosh of olive oil. Rub it all over. Scatter some more spices over the beast, lay it in a roasting pan on a bed of rosemary, and put it in the oven with a splash of water at the bottom of the tin.
- Cook for forty minutes, then lower the heat to 180°C and continue cooking for another two hours, or four if you prefer. If the top blackens, cover it with silver foil. Baste every now and then.
- Rest the meat for twenty minutes before serving.

Cimetiere

Cimetiere armenien

Tsch...

Grand

Fonta...

F...

Cimetiere Catholique

Cimetiere Ottomanes

Reservoir de Pera

Nouvelles Casernes des Artilleurs

Maison de chasse

Ispe...

Hopital des Pestiferes

2 *Aga djamissi* 1

...missi

9

e

0

Galata Serai ...lleges des ...ages

Mosquée

f

Mosquée ...

...ade ...ise

c

Mosquee Khate...

Mosquée

Mosque...

Ottoman

DOLMA = BAGHDJE

Palais de B

Mosquée

Jardin

Mosquée

Abord

uée d'Aoussi Efendi

Courant d'eau

douklu

T H E

The Bellini Card

Venice and Istanbul. Plunder and survival. Their stories entwine across the centuries. So does their food. Yashim's third adventure sends Palewski to Venice, on the trail of a lost portrait. It's a story of false identity, murder and disguise. And eating.

Palewski in his garden

 Palewski lay full-length on a magnificent old carpet. He was propped over a book, wearing a broad-brimmed straw hat and a pair of blue cotton trousers. His feet were bare. A jug and glass of what looked like lemonade stood at his elbow.

'I brought you some ice,' Yashim said. Palewski jumped: he sat up and pushed his hat to the back of his head.

'Ice? Good of you, Yashim.'

Yashim slipped off his shoes and sat down cross-legged on the carpet. Palewski glanced at it. 'Marta laid it out here – she says the sun kills the moth.'

'But you're in the shade.'

'Yes. It was too hot.'

The Bellini Card

LEMONADE
limonata

What could be more refreshing after a trip to market, or when you are lying in the garden with a book?

- Dissolve the sugar in the boiling water. Take it off the heat and add the grated lemon zest.
- Pour the lemon juice into a jug. Strain the cooled sugar water into the jug and mix it with the lemon juice and cold water to taste – probably another ½ litre.
- Refrigerate and serve chilled, with a few leaves of fresh mint.

granulated sugar 225g/8oz
boiling water 250ml/1 cup
zest of a lemon
juice of four lemons
sprig of mint

LAMB AND TOMATO FLATBREADS
lahmacun

Also known as Turkish pizza, lahmacun is a soft thin dough spread with delicious spicy lamb. You can use this recipe to make any size lahmacun you like, four, two, or even a dozen little meze lahmacuns to nibble with drinks.

- Start with the dough. Kickstart the yeast with the sugar in the warm water, and set aside for ten minutes or so until it froths. Put the flour into a mixing bowl, add the salt and yeast and work it until it forms a ball. Knead the ball on a floured surface for five to ten minutes, until it is springy and smooth. Return to the bowl, and cover with a damp cloth somewhere warm.

- For the topping, mix the first seven ingredients together in a bowl. Refrigerate.

- In an hour your dough will have doubled in size. Rub two baking trays with olive oil and put them in the oven, setting it to 220°C. Knock back the dough, knead it briefly on a floured board, and divide it into two, four, or more pieces. Roll and stretch each piece into a circle, pulling the dough with your hands.

- Spread a thin layer of the topping onto each lahmacun, and scatter with the sliced onion and tomato rings. Give them a little drizzle of oil and pop them into the oven as quickly as you can, to stop the heat escaping.

- Check the lahmacun after twenty minutes: the meat should be cooked. Sprinkle them with the parsley, the sumac and a squeeze of lemon, and share them round.

For the flat breads
dried yeast 1 tsp
sugar ½ tsp
warm water 150ml/¾ cup
strong white flour 350g/12 oz
salt ½ tsp
For the topping
olive oil 2 tbsp
pomegranate molasses 2 tbsp
garlic 2 cloves, squashed and chopped with salt
onion 1, grated
minced lamb 250g/½lb
kirmizi biber 2 tsp
chopped fresh mint 2 tsp, or 1 tsp dried
onion 1, sliced into rings
tomatoes 2, sliced into rings
sumac 1 tsp
a bunch of parsley, chopped
lemon 1
salt

"In the Ghetto Popi found firmer footing, where the Jews had been crowded up behind their gates. The air was filled with floating goose down, like a gentle snow, for the people here used goose fat where other Venetians used pork, and it reeked of more than the sewage that offended visitors to Venice elsewhere in the city. It stank of old fish and rags, and the sourness of confined spaces. Napoleon had had the gates demolished, but everyone knew that they still existed in the Venetian mind. A few rich Jews had moved away, and a few — a very few — impoverished gentiles had taken rooms in the Ghetto, but otherwise little had changed in forty years.

Popi stumped along, looking neither left nor right. Something in his manner made the women working in their doorways draw in their feet as he approached; the men shrank to the wall as he passed. It was not that Popi looked official: when the Austrians sent patrols through the streets the people

The air was filled with floating goose down

just watched them go, sullen and unmoving. It was, perhaps, that he came from the other Venice, a Venice that festered beneath the golden afternoon light and the fine tracery of a Byzantine façade, a Venice unimaginative visitors would never penetrate, no matter how much poverty or wretchedness they passed by, trailing their fingertips in the water until their solicitous gondolier hinted that it would be better, perhaps, to keep their hands folded on their laps. How could they, when even the more engaged, more lively minded visitors to the city allowed themselves to be seduced so readily by the prettiness of its whores and the cheapness of its appartamenti?

The people of the Ghetto shrank from Popi as a man of thalers and kreuzers, and of little accounts kept rigorously in black books that had the power to ruin lives.

ROAST GOOSE WITH APPLE SAUCE

Sharing a prohibition on eating pork with Muslims, Mediterranean Jews were very fond of goose. In Christian regions especially they used it for making sausage, salami, and ham, and kept the fat for cooking. This roast goose would have been a Jewish family treat from Ottoman Thessalonica to the southern shores of France.

- Remove the heavy lumps of fat just inside the neck, and prick the bird all over with a fork. Rub the skin with salt and pepper and put the goose breast down on a rack set in a baking tin. Roast for 2½ hours at 220ºC, turning it over halfway through and occasionally pouring off the fat melting into the baking tin. Keep the fat for frying and roasting, and a tablespoonful for the apple sauce.
- Put the spoonful of goose fat, lemon juice, the chopped apple, cinnamon and sugar into a small pan and simmer, covered, until the apple fluffs up. Stir and check for sweetness.

a goose

salt, pepper

juice of ½ lemon

cooking apples 3, peeled, cored and chopped

cinnamon 1½ tsp, ground

sugar 1 tbsp

FISH STEW
karışık deniz ürünleri pilâkisi

This recipe is so delicious and adaptable, you may wonder how you ever cooked fish another way. Don't be afraid of experimenting with the seasonings or the constituent fish and vegetables, either.

- Clean, bone and skin the fish, and cut it into pieces about two inches square. Debeard the mussels. Clean the squid and cut it into rings about ½-inch thick.
- Spread all the ingredients including the fish over the bottom of a roasting pan, scatter with the vegetables, herbs, and spices, and lubricate generously with the oil and wine. The ingredients listed here are only a guide; you could ramp up the garlic, add some sliced peppers, a quarter of a bulb of fennel, sliced, or a few sprigs of parsley or thyme. You could even bury a split lobster in there, if you felt particularly luxurious. Cover the tray with a tight fitting foil lid.
- This can all be done a few hours in advance: put the tray into the fridge and take it out half an hour before you plan to start cooking. Give it a shake before putting it in an oven at 180°C for forty minutes. Everything will be perfectly cooked, and supplied with its own delicious sauce. If you like, you can put the pan on the stove top and reduce the sauce a little more.

mixed fish and shellfish 1kg/2lb *(mussels, clams, white fish, red mullet, squid)*

potatoes 3 medium sized, sliced *about ½ inch thick*

onion or leek 1, chopped

garlic 2 cloves, crushed and roughly chopped

fresh tomatoes 2, roughly *chopped*

a scattering of fresh rosemary

bayleaf

black peppercorns ½ tsp

turmeric ½ tsp

a hefty pinch of salt

olive oil

a splash of white wine or water

Any leftovers, shells removed and the rest gently broken up in the sauce with a wooden spoon, can go to make a spicy fish soup by turning it into a pan with a chopped onion sweated in oil and the tomato sauce on p204, diluted as necessary with white wine and water.

"Yashim took a big lamb's liver and prepared it carefully, removing the arteries and the tough membrane. He sliced it into strips and tossed it in the flour and kirmizi biber.

In the frying pan he sautéed garlic and cumin seeds. The oil was hot; before the garlic could catch he dropped in the sliced liver and turned it quickly with a wooden spoon. The meat tightened and browned; he spooned the slices out and laid them on the onion rings. He chopped some dill and parsley and sprinkled them over the dish, and then, hungry, he took a piece of liver with an onion ring and popped them into his mouth.

Venetians would have cooked the onion until it was very soft. Delicious, in its way, and sweet, but lacking the boldness of the Ottoman original, Yashim thought, as the textures and flavors burst in his mouth. His arnavut cigeri looked better, too.

A shame that he had found no yogurt. He sliced a lemon and laid the wedges around the plate.

He drained the chickpeas. He would cook them with onion, rice, and the remainder of the signora's delicious stock.

He made a marinade with the nigella seeds he had found at the épicier. They had been labeled black cumin, but Yashim knew better. He mixed them with

Into a bowl, weeping, he grated two onions

lemon juice, crushed garlic, salt, pepper, and oregano. Into a bowl, weeping, he grated two onions. He mixed the pulp with a spoonful of salt.

He cleaned his knife and used it to slice three swordfish steaks into chunks, which he turned into the marinade. He took out a stack of vine leaves he had stripped, without much guilt, from a tendril blown over a high garden wall on his way home that morning. He washed them, softened them in the chickpea water in bunches of two or three, and dropped them into a bowl of cold water.

'When you are ready, we can eat,' he announced.

LIVER IN THE VENETIAN MANNER
fegato alla veneziana

This was one of my mother, Jocasta Innes', favourite recipes. She put it in *The Pauper's Cookbook*, and I can't do better than reproduce her version here:

Fried liver and onions is a well-known combination. The Venetian way of preparing it is the nicest of all, the onions stewed very slowly and gently in a little olive oil with the liver – cut into small thin strips – stirred in towards the end.

- Cover the bottom of a heavy frying pan with a thin layer of oil. Put in the onions, and cook gently, covered, for 30-40 minutes, with a little salt and pepper. Meanwhile, with a very sharp knife, shave thinnest possible slices off the liver. If it is calf's liver it will only need 2 or 3 minutes cooking with the onions, but if it is sheep or ox liver you will need to add it to the onions after about half an hour and cook for another 15 minutes.
- You can serve this just as it is, or with plain boiled rice. It is a particularly warming dish in winter.

onions 225g/8oz, finely sliced
liver 125g/4oz (calf's or sheep's preferably)
salt and pepper
oil

I might only add that the liver is easier to shave if it's frozen, or thawing out.

For the same ingredients treated Ottoman style, and equally delicious, see p74.

The Venetian way of slowly cooking onions occurs in the traditional Ottoman dish, Ramadan eggs. They are food fit for a sultan and the next page shows how they are done.

THE SULTAN'S RAMADAN EGGS
Sultan'nın Ramazan yumurtası

In the Yashim short story *The Man Who Stole Puppies* the sultan's mother's recipe for French onion soup reminds Yashim of this excellent dish.

> Up in his apartment, Yashim riddled the stove and set a pan on the coals, for a stock he made with chicken bones and an onion spiced with cloves. He clapped on a lid, blew into his cupped hands, and held them closer to the heat, flexing his fingers.

He peeled and halved the onions, and sliced them thinly on the board while the butter melted in a wide pan. The smell of gently frying onions was always good, like the scent of hot bread, charcoaled meat or crushed mint.

Use milk, George had said: cinnamon and milk. But the validé, the French-born mother of the sultan, had given him another recipe. Sixty years ago she sat on a kitchen table, swinging her legs in the heat of Martinique, while the Creole cook wiped her eyes on her apron and muttered about the way her mama liked it done, with no spice. Simplicity, the validé said, made the soup *haut ton*. And when Yashim asked, she briskly told him onion soup was the only recipe she knew or remembered.

The valide was right, of course: simplicity was *haut ton*. The sultan's eggs were a case in point.

Every year, at the end of Ramadan, the sultan sent for a dish of eggs with onions. There was no trick to the dish, which called for no peculiar ingredients, or fanciful techniques.

The palace chef sliced some onions, very fine, and sweated them in butter for three hours. After that, it was still an easy dish: a splash of vinegar, a pinch of crushed allspice, some sugar, a little salt, and then you made a nest in the jammy onions, and cracked an egg into it, and

sweet onions, 4 large
butter 75g/3oz
allspice 1 tsp, ground
vinegar 1 tbsp
sugar 1 tsp
pinch of salt
eggs 4
vigilance!

put the lid back on.

The egg should be firm, but the yolk could be just a little bit runny...

If the sultan had liked this delicious, but exacting, dish he sent word to confirm that the chef was head of the kitchens, and of the hundreds of chefs who laboured under him.

It was a wise arrangement. Anyone could learn a technique – to clear a soup with egg, say, or spin sugar with a stick – but to make something simple, perfectly – ah! That, Yashim knew, called for vigilance, balance and judgement. Simplicity took real understanding.

The day was fading and Yashim lit the lamps, noticing how the light blossomed in the room and how darkness seemed to rush in against the windows, where the water droplets sparkled on the black glass. He opened a casement a crack, and felt a chill draught.

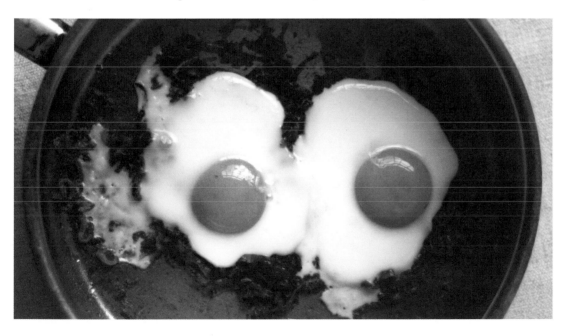

Three hours to make onion jam might not concern a Topkapi chef, but for our purposes an hour with a pinch of salt is long enough to melt the onions into fragrant deliquescence. Keep a lid on the onions while they cook, to trap the moisture.

The Bellini Card

> " The ground floor, lapped by the canal itself, was given over to a quiet and unfashionable café, where watermen sometimes ate their lunch and where Palewski was sure of a dish of rice and a bottle of black wine in the evening.

He wondered what Yashim would make of these risottos, which bore a family resemblance to pilaf, only the rice was thicker. Yashim believed Italians had learned to cook in Istanbul. And certainly the Venetians, who had lived, fought, and traded so much in and around the fringes of the Ottoman world, ate very like the Turks. They had the same particular preferences, Palewski observed, for dozens of little dishes, like meze, though the locals called them *cicchetti* instead, and they were as finicky as any Ottoman about the provenance of certain fruits and vegetables. In Istanbul, one ate cucumbers from Karaköy, or mussels from Therapia. In Venice, Ruggerio insisted that the bitter leaves called radicchio should come from Treviso, the artichokes from Chioggia, and the fresh beans from a little town called Lamon, on the mainland. Neither the Turks nor the Venetians seemed to value fish.

The Venetians, who had lived, fought, and traded so much in and around the fringes of the Ottoman world, ate very like the Turks

GUINEA FOWL WITH PEPPER SAUCE
faraona con la peverada

In mediaeval times, this noble Venetian sauce was made with telltale ingredients such as pomegranate, anchovies and ginger, indicating perhaps an origin in Constantinople, which the Venetians conquered in 1204. The modern version is adapted from a recipe by Gino Santin, founder of Santini's in London's Belgravia and a native of the lagoon.

- Set the oven to 180°C. Make the stuffing by finely chopping the garlic and herbs, then chopping with the onions. Divide it between the two birds, rub them outside with oil and salt, splash with a glassful of wine, and put them in the oven for 25 minutes, breast-down, before turning them the right way up for a further 20 minutes.
- To make the peverada, slice the salami, then stack it and slice it again at right angles, to reduce it to dice. Keep chopping. Chop the liver fine, with the garlic and the parsley. Mix them all in a bowl with the breadcrumbs and the lemon zest.
- Oil the base of a frying pan and gently fry the mixture, until the liver is cooked. Add the lemon juice and some white wine, to make the sauce a little sloppy. Check for seasoning and serve with the roast fowls and slices of polenta (see p124).

garlic 3 cloves
parsley and rosemary mixed handful
onions 3
salt and pepper
guinea fowls 2
olive oil
white wine 100ml/½ cup

Peverada sauce
salami 75g/3oz – ideally a pungent soppressa from the Veneto
chicken livers 75g/3oz
garlic 3 cloves
sprig of parsley
lemon zest 2 tsp, grated
breadcrumbs 50g/2oz
olive oil
juice of a lemon
white wine
salt and pepper

" Yashim found himself watching Signora Contarini as she worked with a short knife, enthroned on a stool by the fire, slicing carrots and onions and garlic against her thumb. She had a knack of slicing the onion so that it remained whole until the last minute, when it cascaded into rings.

One by one she dropped the vegetables into a cauldron set on irons above the fire. The polished stone hearth jutted out into the room; over it, about three feet up, hung a canopy. The smoke drifted lazily upward, some of it escaping into the room to darken the beams and ceiling. The fire itself was small, and the old lady tended it carefully with a poker, now and then tucking back stray twigs and sticks.

When the water came to a boil, the signora carefully unwrapped the beef and lowered it into the cauldron with both hands. Having watched it for a few moments, she went to the table and began to sift through her stores. She shook out a bunch of parsley, folded it, and chopped it finely into a wooden bowl. She cracked a clove from a bulb of garlic, peeled it swiftly, and with little movements of her forefinger sliced it first one way and then the next, before slipping it over and paring it into fragments.

She lifted the lid of a clay jar and fished out a few capers, which she added to the sauce. From another jar she speared a pickled cucumber on the point of her knife and sliced that, too, as she had chopped the garlic.

She put her thumb over the neck of a small green bottle and shook

She worked with a short knife
fire, slicing carrots and onion

a few drops of vinegar into the bowl. A pinch of salt, a round of pepper, and then she began to stir the mixture, adding a thin thread of oil from an earthenware flask until the sauce felt right.

'There must be something I can do to help,. Yashim said. 'Perhaps I could stir the polenta?'

With her eye on the sauce the signora gave an amused grunt: the Moor, stir her polenta?

'I make it *come la seta*,' she said. Like silk. She poured a jug of water into the copper standing beside the fire. 'Talk to your friend, signore.' Yashim moved away politely: he had no wish to put the eye on his hostess's polenta. Maria was sitting by the window, stitching her torn dress. She was wearing the blue bodice and patched grey skirt she had put on before she knew they would be having company.

Yashim glanced back to see the signora threading an endless stream of yellow maize from one hand. The other worked a wooden spoon in slow, firm circles. He smiled and turned his back: in Trabzon, where he was born, the women made kuymak in the same way.

Perhaps they worshipped the same gods, these women, as they performed the daily miracle of transforming the baser elements into silk, the rarest luxury the world could afford.

Maria raised her head from her sewing. 'Some days,' she said in a near whisper, 'we hang an anchovy on a string, above the table. Then we each rub the anchovy on the polenta—and it tastes so good!'

nthroned on a stool by the
nd garlic against her thumb

POLENTA

Polenta should be cooked according the packet instructions, if there are any. In Venice nowadays you can buy it ready made, delicious. Signora Contarini makes it *come la seta*, like silk, by sifting the grains into boiling water and stirring for an hour continuously.

- Boil the salted water. When it simmers, start to sift the polenta through your fingers into the water, stirring all the time. Carry on stirring, like Signora Contarini, for at least half an hour, until the polenta peels in a wedge from the side of the pan.
- Pour out the polenta onto a large lightly oiled chopping board or baking tray. You can dot it with butter and eat straight away or let it set, then grill or bake slices to go with the guinea fowl, on page 121.

salt
water 1¼ litres/2½ pints
polenta (corn meal) 250g/½lb

CRESS SOUP
su teresi çorbası

This recipe is inspired by the light and delicious cooking of Burak Aziz Sürük and Cengiz Çakıt.

- Melt the cress, onion and apple in a pan with the olive oil. Stir in the red lentils and potato, add water, and simmer for 25 minutes. Mash, or whirr in a processor, add salt and pepper, and return to the heat for five minutes.
- Serve with a drizzle of thinned yoghurt, and pepper flakes on the table.

watercress 2 bunches, washed, trimmed and finely chopped
onion 1, diced
green apple 1, peeled, cored, and sliced
olive oil 1 tbsp
red lentils 3 tbsps
potato 1, peeled and diced
water 1.5l/3 pints
salt, pepper
plain yoghurt 150ml/½ cup

SWORDFISH GRILLED IN VINE LEAVES
yaprak sarmalı ızgara kılıç balığı

Beyond the Mediterranean, many humble local fishes grill as well, and taste as good as swordfish. Try wrapping salmon steaks, small mackerel, sardines, or even trout, gutted and scaled, with their heads and tails poking out at either end. Use fig leaves if you like – best blanched briefly first – and any combination of leafy herbs for the dressing.

- The swordfish could use a marinade – mix oil, half the lemon juice, and grated onion with salt and chilli flakes, and let the steaks steep in it for a few hours before you start cooking. Other kinds of fish, if truly fresh, need no preparation.
- Get your grill hot. Bard your fish with oil and lemon, and place each piece on a leaf. Sprinkle a little flaky salt over them, and then wrap the fish up – the swordfish can be packed into a parcel with the ends tucked in, other small fish rolled up like a cigar. Rub the outsides with olive oil.
- Quarter the tomatoes and thread them onto a skewer, with a little salt, and lay them on the grill.
- Lay the fish seam-side down on the hot grill, which will fix the curl of the leaves and stop them unravelling later. Turn them when one side is looking blackened, and cook until done. Transfer to a serving dish.
- Combine the dressing ingredients. Open the parcels and pour the dressing over the fish.

onion 1 large, grated
olive oil
juice of a lemon
swordfish steaks 4
juicy tomatoes 2
salt

For the dressing
a dollop of olive oil
lemon juice
runny honey 1 tsp
pul biber 1 tsp, or hot pepper
fresh herbs a handful, ideally
of dill and parsley

The Bellini Card

WALNUT AND GARLIC SAUCE
tarator

The Ottomans were very fond of trees: it is said that the custom of planting poplars along the roadside, so familiar from driving in France, was adopted from an Ottoman tradition of providing marching armies with decent shade. They loved nut trees, too, and this recipe – for which hazelnuts can substitute for walnuts – is warm, earthy and fabulously versatile. Try it on the side with fish or chicken – or let it take centre stage as a pasta sauce.

- Soak the bread for a minute or two in some of the water. Roughly chop the walnuts. Squeeze the soggy bread and pound it in a mortar with the garlic and walnuts to make a thick paste.
- Add vinegar and a pinch of salt. Drizzle in the oil, pounding and stirring continuously. Use the rest of the water to thin the sauce and keep it creamy. You can also blitz all the ingredients together in a food processor instead. It makes a smoother tarator.
- Scoop the sauce into a bowl and let the flavours develop for a couple of hours, or better still overnight. You can adjust the consistency by beating in a little more water at any time, if you like.

white bread 120g/4oz
water 80ml/⅓cup
walnuts 150g/5oz
garlic 2 cloves, peeled
half balsamic and half wine vinegar or *lemon juice* 3–4tbsp
olive oil 2tbsp
salt

For more delicate fish, steamed, baked or poached, substitute blanched almonds for the walnuts, and lemon juice for the vinegar.

Smiling, almost dancing around the blade, Yashim sliced the onion in half. He sliced each half lengthways and sideways, watching his fingers while he admired the fineness of the blade.

Yashim trims artichokes

He set a pan on the coals, slopped in a gurgle of oil, and dropped in the finely chopped onion. He reached into a crock for two handfuls of rice. He cut the herbs small and scraped them into the rice with the blade.

He threw in a pinch of sugar and a cup of water. The water hissed; he stirred the pan with a wooden spoon. The water boiled. He clapped on a lid and slid the pan to one side.

He began to trim the artichokes. Summer was good. The knife was even better. He smiled as he slid the blade smoothly across the tough tips of the leaves; inside was the choke, which he lifted with a spoon. One by one he dropped the artichokes into the lemony water.

The rice still had bite, and he took it off the heat. As it cooled he ran his thumb down the soft fur inside the bean pods, trying to remember his first meeting with the old calligrapher.

He sighed and dipped a finger into the rice. He took an artichoke out of the water, shook it dry, and stuffed it, scooping up the rice in his fingers and pressing it in. As each one was finished with a little mound of rice, he put it upright in an earthenware crock.

He ran his thumb down the soft fur inside the bean pods

When the crock was full he sprinkled the artichokes with the beans and a few chopped carrots. He drizzled them with oil, around and around, then threw in a splash of water and the rest of the dill and parsley, roughly chopped. Over the top he squeezed another lemon.

He covered the pan with a smaller plate, to weight the artichokes down, and settled the earthenware onto the coals. He set the rice crock on top of the plate. It would be done in an hour or less. He and Malakian would eat it later, cold.

ARTICHOKES WITH BEANS AND ALMONDS
zeytinyağlı kereviz

This says summer – a blindingly delicious meze, or a light lunch. In Mediterranean markets the stallholders stand by their piles of globe artichokes with a knife, swiftly peeling and paring the chokes and tossing them clean into a bucket of lemony salted water. You will need to do the work, maybe in gloves – the leaves can be viciously pointed and sharp.

- Pull off the leaves, cut off the stalks, and pare away the hairy choke with a sharp spoon. Trim off any knobbly bits, rub with the inside of the squeezed lemon and braise them, covered, for 20 minutes in a generous slurp of olive oil, the lemon juice and a splash of water.
- Pod the beans, boil them in salted water for a few minutes, drain and refresh in cold water. Then peel the skins off – nick them and squeeze them at the other side and the naked bean will pop out.
- Put the beans, almonds and the sugar into the pan with the artichokes and simmer for ten minutes longer. Take the pan off the heat, throw in half your dill and let it all cool.
- Take the hearts out and put them on a dish. Stir the chopped tomato into the beans and almonds, and spoon the mixture into the hollows in the middle of the artichokes. Sprinkle the rest of the dill over the dish, and serve at room temperature.

artichokes 4, *large*
olive oil
lemon 1, *juiced*
broad beans 175g/6oz
blanched almonds 75g/3oz
sugar 2 tsp
fresh dill small bunch, chopped
tomatoes 2, peeled and chopped
salt
olive oil

THE ASSASSIN'S STEAK TARTARE

The Tartars were like little brothers to the Ottomans. In wartime they rode on their hardy steppe ponies deep into enemy territory, sometimes as far as the banks of the Rhine. On these journeys they galloped without pause until, at a signal from their khan, they wheeled round and began making for their homeland in the Crimea, loading themselves with slaves and booty. They cured meat under their saddles, pounding it soft and fine, which they devoured raw. Get your beef absolutely fresh from a reputable butcher.

For four assassins:

- The bacteria that might kill you lies on the outer surface of the meat, so having bought your fillet you must take a very sharp knife and boldly slice away its outer edges all round.
- Start afresh with a clean board and a clean knife. If you have a mezzoluna, so much the better. Chop the herbs and vegetables very fine. Sprinkle them with salt, and put them into a bowl.
- Set the steak on the board and slice it as fine as you can, across the grain to begin with. Stack the slices together, squeeze them lightly, then slice them again, lengthways. Turn the board ninety degrees and press the fillet strips together again – they are almost as soft as putty, and cut smoothly when they are squeezed together. So finally cut them up in the opposite direction, as small as you can. Don't mash them: you want soft crumbs of steak, not a paste.
- Slide the chopped steak into the bowl with the herbs, chilli and vegetables, and mix well. Check for salt.
- Scoop the steak tartare onto a plate, and make a depression at the top with the back of a soup spoon. Separate an egg yolk from the white and tip the yolk into the dip.
- Grind black pepper over the plate. It's very good with toast.

fillet of beef 250g/8oz
banana shallot 1, *small*
cornichons 4
capers 1 tbsp (rinsed if salted)
parsley ½ tbsp
tomato 1
pul biber ½ tsp, *or a fresh chilli, deseeded*
pinch of salt
egg yolk 1
black pepper

" Yashim tensed his stomach. His shoulders bunched.

And he jacknifed. He took a step forward, his shoulders dropped, and he doubled at the waist.

He sensed, rather than felt, the blade slicing through the soft skin behind his ear.

He kicked back abruptly with one leg.

His hope was that the Tartar had lost form: killing Venetians was like liming a tree for birds.

His foot connected, but not hard: the next moment, the Tartar had a grip of his ankle. Left hand – Yashim wrenched himself forwards and took a mouthful of the bed.

With both hands on the mattress he launched himself backwards.

The Tartar sidestepped easily, but now Yashim was at his back. As the Tartar whipped round, Yashim flung out one fist, and then the other: the raised knuckle of his middle finger sank into the Tartar's cheek.

The Tartar had him by the scruff of his neck; Yashim felt himself choke, and flailed blindly.

The Tartar sidestepped easily, but Yashim was at his back

Then the Tartar seized his waistband and with a grunt sent him crashing through the air – Yashim raised his hands and the shutters burst apart like rotten twigs.

But Yashim was already twisting as he flew: his knees doubled against the windowsill and for a second he saw the dark bulk of buildings swing upwards. His head cracked against the wall – in a moment the Tartar would flip his feet through the window, and he would be gone.

Instinctively, Yashim tensed his legs. With a final effort he jerked himself upright: the Tartar was at the window.

Yashim grabbed him with both hands – but the momentum was too feeble to carry him back into the room. As he fell again back he kicked out, spinning them both into space, precipitating the Tartar over and over into the air.

Only in Venice would anyone survive a two-storey drop.

The Tartar smacked into the water first. Yashim seemed to pummel in on top of him – and was thrashing and coughing, as he came up for air.

He kicked out, in panic: the Tartar was still beneath the water.

Nothing happened. Yashim scudded back, towards the security of the palazzo wall; and it was there, in the faint glow of lamplight on the water, that he saw the Tartar break the surface ten yards away.

He was swimming away, up the Canal.

Yashim wished he could let him go.

He wiped his mouth with his fingers, and tasted blood.

With his other hand he found the knife. The knife that Malakian had given him for an aspre: the cook's knife.

A knife that a hunter might carry, too, for slipping off a pelt.

The knife that was made of Damascene.

Yashim kicked off from the wall, and began to hunt.

There is a - suitably byzantine - connection with Venice. A Piedmontese version of steak tartare, known as *carne cruda all'Albese*, inspired Giuseppe Cipriani, the owner of Harry's Bar in Venice, to create a raw beef dish for the contessa Amalia Nani Mocenigo in 1963. He called it *carpaccio* after the Venetian painter known for his characteristic palette of red and white. It is done by shaving the thinnest possible slices off a piece of fillet or sirloin. It helps if the meat is partially frozen first. Serve with salt and black pepper, a drizzle of olive oil and rocket.

HOT SAUCE
acı sos

From the *harissa* of Tunisia, to the *adjika* of Georgia, every region of the old empire has a variant of hot chilli sauce. Arabian and Georgian versions use coriander leaves.

Stir this into a stew, use it as a marinade for roast chicken...the permutations are endless. It lives for a week or two in a jar in the fridge.

- Quarter the tomato and put it on a baking tray with the pepper and the chilli, if fresh; dried chillis need to be soaked in a little boiling water instead. Bake in a hot oven 200°C. After twenty minutes take out the pepper and put it under a tea towel. In a few minutes the skin will be ready to peel away. Discard skin and seeds, and put the flesh in a bowl.
- Take fresh chillis, if using, out of the oven and sweat them under the cloth for five minutes. Rub the skin off the tomato, skin the chillis, squeeze out their seeds, and put them in a bowl with the pepper. Add the dried chillis whole, if using.
- Toast the coriander and cumin seed in a dry pan, while you peel and smash the garlic in a little salt.
- In a mortar, grind the toasted spice, then add the garlic and mash it into a paste. Alternatively you can whizz everything together in a processor. If you are using pestle and mortar, add the chilli and the pepper to the spicy garlic. When they are roughly pulped, add the tomato and pulverise. Don't overdo it, if you want to keep some texture in the sauce.
- Put the mixture into a bowl and finish with a spoonful of oil, and lemon juice.

tomato 1
red pepper 1
red chillis 2, *or 4 dried chillis*
coriander seed 1 *tsp*
cumin seed 1 *tsp*
garlic 3 *cloves*
pinch of salt
olive oil
lemon juice 1 *tsp*

Mosquée du Sultan Selim

Imprimerie

Plantations
nouvelles

Hôpital

Kawak Iskelessi

Maison des Bostan

KAWAK

Caserne

Couven

Mosquée de Ka

Harem Iskelessi

Abord dangereux

Saghardjiler B

An Evil Eye

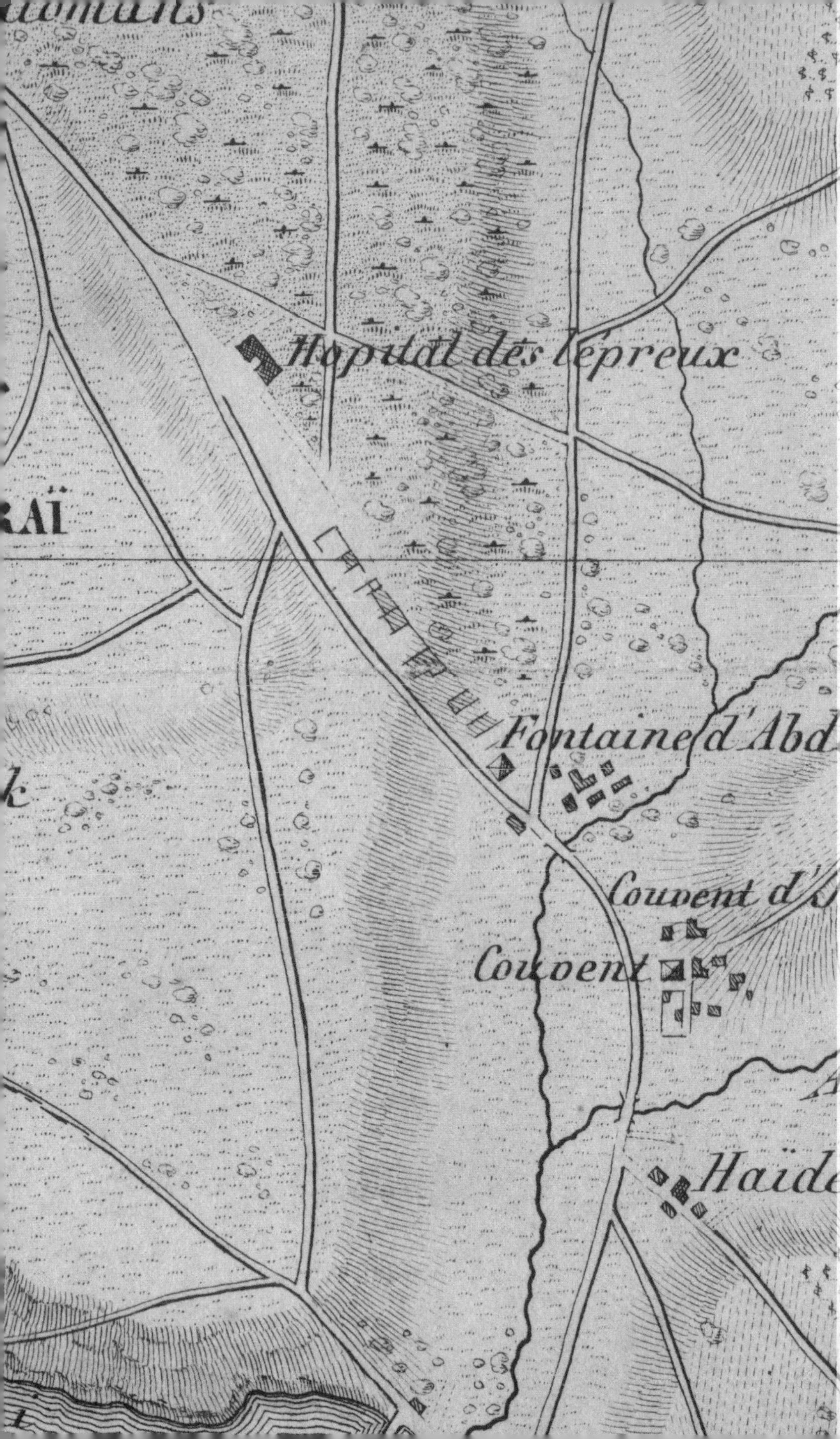

Hôpital des lepreux

RAï

Fontaine d'Abdoulah

Couvent d'Ibrahim

Couvent

Aynli

Haïder Pasch

The fourth Yashim adventure sees him back in Istanbul, and in the sultan's harem. It's a winter book, which includes plenty of seasonal dishes, and the odalisques drinking soup by a fire, under a thick quilt.

" 'One by one, along the edge of the Golden Horn, the little fishing boats drawn up on the strand lit their lamps as dusk descended over the Bosphorus. Dark figures crouched beneath the boats' prows, tending the little braziers where they cooked their fish: mackerel, mostly, headed, gutted and then split apart to sizzle for a few minutes over the glowing charcoal. The cold, damp air reeked of the oil that dripped into the fires.

A swarthy Nubian sailor slapped his hams and squatted down by one of the braziers. The fisherman took his coin, and turned a hot mackerel fillet into a flat roll.

Overhead, in the branches of a wintry plane tree, Kadri licked his lips, and waited.

An Evil Eye

PIDE

You have all this great food, and you're throwing a party. But there's something missing. It's bread. Fluffy, hollow pita bread, for stuffing and mopping and chewing.

- Stir the yeast in a cup with 100ml (½ cup) of warm water and a pinch of sugar, and set it aside until it foams. Mix the flour, salt and the rest of the sugar in a bowl, then pour in the yeast. Start mixing the dough, adding a little more warm water at a time, until you have a solid ball, as dry as it can be without falling apart.

- Work the dough on a clean surface, as hard as you can for as long as you can, then add the oil and knead it in well. Keep the faith: your dough will eventually become elastic and smooth.

- At that point you can either put it in a bowl in the fridge, covered with cling film, for baking the next day, or if you want pita bread today, leave it to stand at room temperature for about an hour.

- Now is the time to turn your oven up really high.

- Roll your dough into a sausage and cut it into 12 pieces. Roll them tightly into balls and lay them on a lightly floured tray – they will rise, so set them well apart from each other. Give them anything from 15-30 minutes, depending on the warmth of the kitchen, while you put a heavy baking tray in the middle of the oven.

- Roll out each ball on a floured surface, using your rolling pin in different directions to get them down to ¼-inch thick.

- As fast as you can, whisk open the oven door and flick as many pitas as will fit onto the tray. Shut the door quickly – you want to keep the heat in.

- They take two or three minutes to puff up and cook, no more. Don't let them brown.

- Take them out, put in the next batch, and stack the puffy pitas under a slightly damp cloth. Eat them as soon as you can – or let them cool and freeze them.

dried yeast 2tsp
warm water 400ml/¾ pint
sugar 1 tsp
strong white flour 500g/1lb
salt 1½ tsp
olive oil 2 tbsp

An Evil Eye

" Yashim laid the ingredients out on the chopping board: onion, garlic, a long red chili, and a carrot that the man had scraped clean. He set the sultan's pan on a gentle heat and covered its base with olive oil, adding a small knob of butter before he chopped the onion into very small pieces.

The knife, he noticed, was as keen as his own, and heavier: it would split a silk scarf.

Finding himself in the greatest kitchen in Istanbul, Yashim set about making one of the simplest dishes he knew: lentil soup.

He scraped the seeds out of the chili and chopped it together with the garlic, admiring the balance of the knife and the slight feathered curve toward its tip. The butter had melted; he

He set the sultan's pan on a gentle heat

shook the pan and swept in the vegetables, with a big pinch of cumin and coriander.

He cut the carrot into small dice, and stirred it into the onions as they began to turn.

The cook passed him a small brass grinder. Yashim smelled the fenugreek: he gave it a few twists and handed it back.

'Thank you,' he said. 'You have the lentils?'

The cook nodded. He handed Yashim a cup of lentils, which he poured into the pan like a cascade of treasure, stirring them around for a few moments with a small spoonful of white sugar.

The cook brought him a bowl of the clarified stock.

Yashim smiled. 'When you like,' he said; and then: 'enough.' The steam rose in a puff, and drifted into the vast cool vaults overhead. 'Now, a lid—and I'll help you with the carrots, if you like.'

When the soup was done, Yashim ladled it into a bowl and sprinkled it with chopped parsley.

He put a bowl over the top, to keep it warm, and carried it carefully back to the harem.

LENTIL SOUP
kırmızı mercimek çorbası

This was the first dish I was ever taught in Istanbul – by Hande Bözdogan, founder of the Istanbul Culinary Institute, no less. It's delicious. She – like Yashim – cooks it like this.

- Melt the butter in a saucepan, and gently soften the onions to translucency. Stir in the garlic, potato and cumin, then add the lentils, salt, pepper and stock. Simmer for 25 minutes, covered, until the lentils are soft. You can run the soup through a blender or leave it as it is.
- Heat the oil in a frying pan, turn the mint and hot pepper together in the oil, and sprinkle it over the soup.

butter *75g/3oz*

onions *2, finely chopped*

garlic *2 cloves, finely chopped*

potato *1, peeled and grated*

cumin *½ tsp, ground*

red lentils *200g/8oz*

chicken or meat stock *1.5 litres/3 pints*

salt, pepper

olive oil

mint *small bunch fresh, or 1 tbsp dried*

pul biber *1 tsp*

" Yashim tipped a basket of peppers onto the bench where he worked, the long peppers shaped like slippers, pale green and subtly aromatic.

'If your hands are clean, Kadri, you might wash the peppers,' he suggested. He set the kettle to boil, and meanwhile poured a pint of white wine vinegar into a bowl, in which he dissolved a couple of spoonfuls of salt, and let it stand.

He sliced a few carrots and broke out the cloves from two heads of garlic, brushing away the dry skin but leaving the cloves intact. In deference to George's unexpected enthusiasm, he had bought tomatoes; they had discussed the question, and George had agreed to supply him the tomatoes green and still hard, as unripe as the apricots he always used. Ripe tomatoes, Yashim insisted, would spoil the crunchiness of the pickle. Finally, he took a pointed cabbage and tore it into pale shards.

On the bench he lined up his jars, all French, with tight-fitting lids, imported by English merchants and sold in the Egyptian bazaar; Yashim used earthenware crocks, too, which were cheaper — but pickles winking behind glass were irresistible, like a warm fire on a cold night.

He sluiced the jars with boiling water and began to pack them, laying the peppers and the other vegetables on a carpet of cabbage leaves, alternating the layers as he filled the jars. When they were full, he used a wooden spoon to press the layers down, satisfied by the sound of crisp vegetables creaking and snapping.

'Now, Kadri, the vinegar.'

Kadri poured carefully, his tongue between his teeth, until the vegetables in each jar were completely submerged. To make sure, Yashim dropped a small ceramic disc on top, to weight everything down; then he screwed on the lids.

'It'll be good," he said. "But not for a few weeks yet. We'll make something quicker, too. Can you shell those peas?'

THREE PICKLES

Ottoman pickles can be made to store, bringing a glint of fairground colour to the larder, or made a day or so in advance, using less vinegar: either way the vegetables are eaten cold and they're crunchy and delicious. They enliven any cold collation: try them in sandwiches, with salads and cheese, or as a simple meze, with raki. Pickles are also traditionally eaten with *fasulye* (see p190).

In Istanbul, people go to pickle shops for a glass of pickling juice: very healthy.

PINK TURNIP PICKLE
turp turşusu ve şalgam suyu

This pickle is a gorgeous shade of pink and so good it can be eaten on its own, as a little meze to go with an evening drink. The recipe was known in the 15th century, around the time of the Ottoman conquest of Istanbul.

- Peel and quarter the turnips, peel and slice the beetroot, and stack them in a clean jars with the sliced garlic. Boil the water with the salt and vinegar until the salt has dissolved, and pour it over the turnips. Make sure the vegetables are completely covered by adding more boiling water if necessary. Seal the jars and let them cool.

small turnips 1kg/2lb
beetroot 1
garlic 3 cloves, sliced
water 850ml/1¾ pints
salt 2½ tbps
white wine vinegar 3 tbsp

SOUR-SWEET QUICK PICKLE
acı ve tatlı turşu

- Beat the honey into the vinegar until dissolved, and add the oil.
- Cut your vegetables into bite-sized pieces. Blanch vegetables like cauliflower, carrot and cabbage in boiling water for 30 seconds, then refresh under the cold tap and shake them dry. Leeks, courgettes, green beans and peppers can go raw into the jar, with the celery.
- Pack a scalded jar with the vegetables, top up with the pickling liquid, and seal.
- Keep the jar in the fridge for at least two days, and serve as a meze salad with olive oil, salt and chopped coriander.

runny honey 100ml/3oz
white wine vinegar 600ml/1¼ pints
olive oil 200ml/½ pint
your five preferred vegetables 100g/4oz each
a celery stick, sliced fine

QUICK PICKLE
turşu

All the deliciousness of pickled vegetables – but ready to eat in a few days. Pack a large jar with an assortment of vegetables, cut into nibble-sized pieces, along with a couple of bayleaves and some garlic cloves, sliced. Drop in a dried, or fresh sliced chilli if you like. You could use cauliflower, turnip, fennel, carrots, French beans, peas, peppers, chillis and even cabbage, in any variety you choose. You can sling everything into the jar or spend a happy afternoon slicing and arranging the pieces artistically.

- Make a brine by boiling 3 tbsp of salt to every litre of water, along with a handful of peppercorns and coriander seeds, and a star anise. Boil for a few minutes, until the salt has dissolved, pour over the vegetables, and seal.

salt

chopped vegetables a medley

bayleaves

garlic 2-3 cloves

fresh or dried chilli, whole

peppercorns 1tsp

coriander seeds 1tsp

star anise 1

To make a pickle you can store for longer, replace 250ml of the salted water with white wine vinegar, and boil in the same way. You may prefer it more vinegary, and less salty: I do.

An Evil Eye

Tuna in oil
ton balığı

Everything is good, in good oil, stewed slowly. The Greeks do it – mushrooms *a la Grecque* are stewed in oil, gently, with a clove of garlic. The leeks in oil, on p163, are equally good to have about. You can turn tuna steaks into a delicious meze which will keep for several days in the fridge, and can be eaten at room temperature, if you can avoid eating them hot, with fried potatoes. The oil itself will be fabulous to use later, maybe for a seafood pilaf or for *kakavia* (see p154). Or simply drizzle it over a fillet of fish, add a few chopped herbs, wrap in foil and bake in the oven... When mackerel are in season, and you can get them really fresh, their fillets make a delicious alternative to tuna.

- Halve the steaks, and turn them in the mixture of cumin, pepper, sugar, salt and a bit of oil, in an ovenproof dish. Let them marinade for half an hour.
- Grate the zest of the lemon and sprinkle it over the steaks. Pour the juice of the lemon over them, and add oil until they are nearly submerged. Give them a generous twist of black pepper and clap a tight lid on the dish, or cover with foil.
- Put in a very low oven for half an hour or more, until the tuna sets, and is cooked through. 140ºC is fine, Gas 1. They'll be delicious hot with a green salad and some plain rice.

tuna steaks 4
cumin seeds, isot biber 1 tsp each
black pepper
fine caster sugar 1 tbsp
salt 1 tbsp
lots of olive oil
lemon 1

PALACE FIG PUDDING
incir tatlısı

This pudding dish was a palace staple, very easy on the chef but utterly delicious – especially made with soft dried figs available particularly to sultans.

* With the stem uppermost, cut each fig horizontally almost in half, without actually severing them.
* Soak the figs in warm water for 30 minutes. Save the water.
* Break the walnut halves into pieces, not too small, and stuff some into the middle of each fig. Close the figs and stand them side by side in a shallow saucepan.
* Stir the sugar into the warm figgy water and pour it over the figs, with the cinnamon sticks and a small pinch of salt. Set on a high heat and bring the liquid to the boil, then lower the heat and simmer the figs gently for 20 minutes or so, covered, until the liquid is syrupy. Let them cool.
* Serve the figs at room temperature, with the syrup drizzled on top and a sprinkling of chopped walnuts.

dried figs 12
warm water 350ml/1½ cups
walnuts 12, halved
sugar 400g/14oz
cinnamon 2 sticks
pinch of salt
chopped walnuts 120g/1 cup
cream or yoghurt

Double cream, clotted cream, whipped cream, yoghurt and ice cream all go with them, very well.

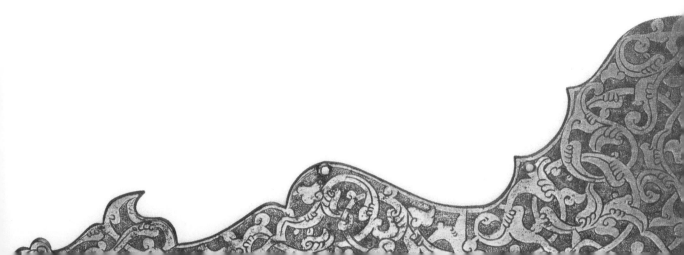

66 They wandered off along the track that lined the shore, overhung with Judas trees. Small fishing boats with painted eyes were drawn up on the beach, watching them as they passed. On the rocks, fishermen sat mending their nets or cleaning the day's catch.

Yashim sniffed the air.

'That smells good, my friends!'

A group of fishermen were sitting around a fire and dipping bread into a cauldron. 'You are very welcome, kyrie. Join us. Take some bread, and have a little wine.'

An older man, with a fine crop of white curls, grinned and winked at Palewski. 'For the Frankish kyrie, the wine is good.'

Yashim squatted gravely by the fire. Palewski settled like a cormorant on a rock. A boy was sent to the sea with a couple of tin plates. He presented them, clean and fresh, to the newcomers. The old fisherman ladled out some stew, and someone passed them a loaf of round bread, from which they broke pieces.

Palewski held his thimble of yellow wine to the light. 'To your hospitality.' He drank; the men murmured their approval; his glass appeared refreshed.

Yashim was curious to taste the fishermen's stew. He took several mouthfuls: it was strong, flavored with the wild thyme that grew farther up the shore, beyond the track.

'Tomato!' he exclaimed.

One of the younger men nodded. 'I've seen them growing it, kyrie. It grows like a weed, when you know *"I think tomato is good to eat."* how, and it tastes good. Even raw.'

The old fisherman put up a stubby finger. 'Raw, it's no good.' He passed his hand across his belly. 'It lies here, very cold. And gives my wife headache.'

'She always has headache.'

'Not like this.'

A stew on the rocks

'What do you think, kyrie?'

'I think tomato is good to eat.' Yashim picked out a little mass of bones with his fingers, and cast them toward the sea. 'But like an aubergine, it is dangerous raw.'

The old man nodded. Palewski said, in his workmanlike Greek, 'I have read that it is safe to eat it raw, but you should not eat the . . . the little seeds.'

'The pips, that's right. That's where the trouble lies.'

The younger man shrugged amiably. 'I eat it, pips and all.' He touched the knuckle of his thumb to his belly. 'I feel good.'

'Why not? You're young.'

Yashim smiled and buried his head in his plate. Greeks always had some opinion, and they adored novelty. Their conversation never flagged.

KAKAVIA

The Ottomans used to say, 'God had made the earth for their Dominion, and Enjoyment, and the sea only for Christians.' They meant that while the Turks farmed, herded and won important battles, the Greeks went fishing. This was the simple stew Greek fishermen might make when the boats came in, the Ottoman equivalent of bouillabaisse.

In *An Evil Eye*, the cooking of kakavia sparks a discussion of tomatoes, whether they are good for you or not. Unknown to the Ottoman kitchen in 1800, by 1900 tomatoes had got into almost everything, and it is hard to imagine Mediterranean food without them. Which makes me wonder if, in the olden days, fishermen flavoured their kakavia with sour little wild greens picked on the shore instead of tomatoes.

You create a fish stock, gently fry some alliums, and combine them with the fish. It's catch-of-the-day stuff, with nothing set in stone, but avoid oily fish like salmon or mackerel.

- Fishmongers always have 'frames', meaning heads, bones and all that's left of a fish after the fillets have been taken, and they may even give them away. To make the stock, cover the frames with water, add a pinch of salt, peppercorns and the bayleaf, and bring to gentle simmer. 20 minutes simmering is enough.
- Use a heavy-bottomed pan, like a casserole, to melt the onion in olive oil until it turns clear. Add the garlic and the potato, stir in the tomatoes, and let it soften. Imagine, if you like, that you are a fisherman on the shore, casting about for anything tasty to go in the pot. Chilli fresh or flaked, chopped leek, a sprig of fresh thyme – they will be good, if you have them.
- Look to your fish. You might have mullet, cod, hake or bass

For the fish stock
fish frames
water 2 1/4 pints
salt
peppercorns 1 tsp
bay leaves

in any combination, but try to keep a mix of fish; have it filleted – skinned, too, if you like – and cut the pieces at least an inch square, or bigger.

- When the stock is done, strain it into the pot – all hissing steam and then a comfortable bubble. Use as much stock as you want, depending how soupy you'd like this kakavia to be. I make it thick, so that it can be soaked up with bread.

- Lower the pieces of fish into the stewing pan and simmer them for about ten minutes, till done but not collapsing. Add mussels five minutes before the end, if you use them.

- Good bread, squeeze of lemon, salt and pepper on the table.

- Καλη ορεξη! Bon appetit...

onions 2, *sliced*
olive oil
head of garlic, *peeled and crushed*
potato 1, *thickly sliced*
tomatoes 2 or 3, *chopped*
chilli
leek
thyme
mixed fish 1kg/2lb (mullet, cod, hake etc)
a handful of shellfish
lemon
salt, pepper

“For Yashim, too, the interview provided an opportunity, for as his caïque returned him to Istanbul, it overhauled a fishing boat bringing in the morning's catch. Back at his apartment, Yashim laid two mackerel on the board. He liked all fish, but mackerel was best: he always liked a mackerel sandwich off the boats that drew up along the Golden Horn in the evening, grilling their fish on shallow braziers along the shore.

Today, he had more elaborate plans.

Taking the sharp kitchen knife an Armenian friend had given him, he made a tiny incision below the gills of each fish. Through the narrow opening he drew out the guts, taking care not to widen the little cuts any further, then he rinsed the fish and laid them back on the board.

He dropped a handful of currants into a bowl and covered them with warm water from the kettle.

With a rolling pin he rolled and bashed the mackerel from the gills to the tail. He snapped the backbones two or three times along their length, pinching the fish between his fingers until the skin was loose. Carefully he began to empty the skin, squeezing the flesh and the bones through the tiny openings.

He picked up the two skins, each still attached to its head and tail, and rinsed them out.

He dried his hands, and peeled and chopped a few shallots. While they softened in the pan, he crushed peeled almonds and walnuts with the rolling pin, chopped them fine with the knife, and stirred them into the shallots with a handful of pine nuts. As they colored he added the currants and a handful of chopped dried apricots. He put cinnamon, allspice berries, and a pinch of cloves into his grinder and ground them over the nuts, adding a dash of kirmizi biber, or black charred chili flakes.

He scraped the flesh from the fish bones and tossed it into the pan with a pinch of sugar.

Yashim stuffs mackerel

FOR STUFFED MACKEREL, SEE THE NEXT PAGE

He chopped parsley and dill, split a lemon, and squeezed it over the stuffing.

It smelled good already. He took a nibble, sprinkled the mix with a pinch of salt and black pepper, then stirred it and took it off the heat.

He scraped the flesh from the fish bones and tossed it into the pan with a pinch of sugar

When it was cool, he stuffed the mixture back into the mackerel skins, squeezing and patting them to restore their shape.

He laid a wire grill over the coals, scattered the fish with flour and oil from his fingers, and laid them on the wire, turning them as they spat and sizzled.

Meanwhile, he sharpened his knife on a stone.

When the mackerel skin was bubbling and lightly browned, he took the fish from the heat and sliced them thickly on the board. Very carefully, he slid the fish onto a plate.

An Evil Eye

SPICED STUFFED MACKEREL
uskumru dolması

Here are instructions for Yashim's recipe on the previous page. This is pure Istanbul – snazzy and delicious. These days the mackerel sold in Istanbul fishmarkets is mostly Norwegian, but if you can source it really fresh there is no other fish to beat it. You want a large mackerel for this bejewelled feast, or it will get too fiddly.

- First make the stuffing. Chop the shallots up fine, and sweat them in olive oil in a frying pan. Add the three kinds of nuts. As they begin to colour, throw in the currants, apricots, spices, kirmizi biber and sugar and mix well. Slide the pan off the heat while you prepare the fish.
- With the mackerel belly up, use a sharp knife to make an incision behind the gills, keeping the backbone and head intact and attached. Remove the guts with your fingers through the opening, and rinse the mackerel under the tap.
- Lay the mackerel on a board and beat it lightly with a rolling pin, or an empty bottle, making sure you break the backbone into pieces. Massage the skin gently, to loosen it from the flesh. Working from the tail towards the head, squeeze the flesh and bones out through the incision below the gills.
- It is not easy. Go gently, trying not to tear the skin, as if you were squeezing a tube of toothpaste. You are left with an empty skin, still attached to the head. Rinse it out.
- Pick the bones from the meat and discard them. Fold the meat gently into the stuffing mixture, cooking for a minute

For the stuffing
shallots 4-5
olive oil
pine nuts 2 tbsp
blanched almonds 2 tbsp, slivered
walnuts 3 tbsp, finely chopped
currants 1-2 tbsp, soaked in warm water for ten minutes and drained
dried apricots 6-8, finely chopped
cinnamon 2 tsp, ground
allspice 1 tsp, ground
cloves ½ tsp, ground
kirmizi biber 1 tsp, or ½ tsp *chilli powder*
sugar 1 tsp

or two before adding the herbs, the lemon juice, and salt
and pepper to taste.

- Let the mixture cool a bit. Holding the mackerel's head
  back, use a teaspoon to fill the empty skin, shaking and
  squeezing the stuffing right down to the tail-end. It looks
  like a mackerel again.
- You can roll the fish in flour and fry it, or brush with oil
  and set it under the grill, hot, until the skin begins to
  blister.
- Finally, with a very sharp knife, slice the mackerel thickly,
  lay it on a plate like the fish it is, and serve with lemon
  wedges.

fresh mackerel, *1 large*
dill *and* **parsley** *small bunches,*
finely chopped
juice of 1 lemon
plain flour
sunflower oil
salt and pepper

Pan fried Turbot
kalkan balığı tavası

Starting the day before, this is a palace refinement designed to heighten the flavour of this palatial fish, which it does in a deliciously scented way. It works well with brill and halibut, too.

- Add 2 tsp salt to the water, and the saffron, and stir to dissolve the salt.
- Gut and wash the turbot.
- Slice the lemons thinly, and line a dish big and deep enough to hold the turbot and the water with half the slices.
- Lay the turbot on top, and sprinkle it with salt. Cover the fish with the remaining lemon slices, and gently pour in the salted saffron water.
- Cover with greaseproof paper held down with a plate or a lid, and leave it overnight in the fridge.
- When it comes to cook, remove the turbot from the marinade and pat it dry. Melt the butter, or warm the oil, in a frying pan and fry the fish brown on both sides.

salt
water *1litre/2 pints*
saffron *a pinch*
turbot *1*
lemons *4*
butter *80g/3oz, or* *olive oil*
2tbsp

LEEKS IN OIL
zeytinyağlı pırasa

It's a very good thing to have a dish of lemony leeks in the larder. They go well with salads and in sandwiches, or simply on their own, as a meze or as an accompaniment to some bigger dish.

- Trim the leeks, split in two lengthways, wash out the soil from the leafy end, and split again across the grain.
- Put them at the bottom of a saucepan with a generous coating of olive oil and a sprinkling of salt. Wash, peel and slice the carrots diagonally, ¼ inch thick, and push them down to nestle among the leeks. Set the pan on a low heat, with a lid on, and sweat them for 20 minutes.
- If you wish to use rice, you can sprinkle it over the leeks at this point, with 100ml water. Give them a shake and continue cooking for half an hour. If you aren't using rice, keep the lid on and keep sweating the leeks until they're soft – ten minutes or so.
- Take them off the heat, lift the lid and squeeze half a lemon over the leeks. Serve cold.

leeks 1kg/2lb

carrots 2–3

olive oil

salt

water

uncooked rice 3 tbsps
(optional)

lemons

RUBY PILAF
pancarlı pilav

Palace communications were traditionally bound in vermilion silk ribbon, the very colour of this pilaf, which looks sensational.

- Boil the beetroots whole, until tender. Pick them out of the water and let them cool, reserving the water which will be a dark ruby red. Rub the beetroot skins off – wear gloves if you don't want your hands stained red – and chop the beetroot roughly into 1cm cubes.
- Soak the rice in warm water for half an hour, and wash it until the water runs clear. Drain as well as you can. Melt the onions in butter. When they are soft, add the rice.
- After a couple of minutes add enough of the beetroot water to cover the rice and a little more. Turn up the heat and after five to eight minutes, or when the stock has all been absorbed, check the rice; it should be a little nutty, but almost ready. If necessary add a little more stock and continue cooking until the rice is almost done.
- Gently stir in the chopped beetroot, with butter dotted over the top of the rice.
- Cover the pan with a cloth and a lid. Over a whisper of heat, or none, let the rice steam for fifteen minutes.
- Turn the rice out into a dish, helping to fluff it out with a fork.

beetroot 250g/8oz, boiled and boiling water reserved
basmati rice ½ kg/1lb, rinsed and drained
onion 1, finely chopped
butter 1tbsp
salt
chicken stock or water

"Yashim clapped his book shut with an exclamation of surprise. 'Everything that is useful,' Gautier had written, 'is ugly.'

Yashim reads a French book

Yashim shook his head. What sad world did this Gautier inhabit, that everything useful could be described as ugly? It was a fault of the Franks to make their slightest opinions sound like revealed laws, of course. He contemplated the nutcracker in his hand, with its chased brass handles and polished iron jaws. He let his eyes wander around the apartment, from the shelf beside the divan, with its collection of porcelain and books, to the stack of crocks and pans in the far corner where he cooked.

At his thigh were a marble mortar and the knife with *Ammar made me* inscribed on the Damascus blade. These useful things, Yashim felt, were also beautiful. With half-closed eyes he thought about Istanbul, with its lovely minarets for calling the people to prayer. He thought of the scalloped and fluted fountains, which relieved the people's thirst. He considered the slender caïques,

These useful things, Yashim felt, were also beautiful

which bustled people across the water in all directions. Surely no one thought them ugly!

He cracked another walnut, smiling as his thoughts turned to the sultan's palace. The loveliest women that the empire could provide— would Gautier call them useless, then? Yashim knew the harem as a school, an arena for ambition, a human factory geared to the production of royal heirs. Many a pasha had blessed the Circassian girls for drawing a headstrong sultan away from delicate affairs of state and into their beds. The mere effort of observing the intricate etiquette of the harem quarters was enough to keep a sultan busy.

Gautier, he felt, had got it the wrong way around.

Yashim laid the book on the divan, careful not to let his oily fingers stain the green leather binding with walnut juice.

Yashim took the mortar to his kitchen, set it on the bench, and put a small open pan on the coals. He began to pound the walnuts with a stone pestle. When the pan was hot he threw in a scattering of cumin seeds. He rattled the pan on the coals and poured the seeds into a black iron grinder. He turned the handle and ground the cumin over the walnuts. He added a pinch of kirmizi biber, which he had made in the autumn. He sprinkled the end of a dry loaf with water, then carried on pounding the walnuts. Eventually he squeezed the bread dry and crumbled it into the mortar between his fingers, along with a generous dollop of pomegranate molasses.

When the muhammara was finely pounded, he stirred a thread of olive oil into the mix. He tasted the purée, added a pinch of salt and a twist of pepper, and poured it into a bowl, which he covered with a plate and set to one side.

For the next hour he worked at his remaining meze: a light salad of beans and anchovies mixed with slices of red onion and black olives, and another made with grated beetroot and yogurt. Finally, he made soup with leeks and dill.

He was almost done when there was a knock on the door. A chaush in palace uniform stood at the top of the stairs, carrying an invitation on vermilion paper.

The chief black eunuch requested Yashim's presence at the Besiktas palace that afternoon.

Yashim bowed, placed a hand to his chest, and murmured: 'I shall attend, inshallah.'

CUCUMBER WITH YOGHURT
cacık

I like the casual generosity of cacık, which can appear as a meze, to be eaten with bread, or as a side-dish with, say, grilled meat – or be diluted to make a refreshing cold summer soup.

- Grate the cucumber into a colander, set the colander on a plate, and sprinkle the cucumber with a teaspoonful of salt. Leave it to drain its liquid for a few hours, or overnight, under a plate as a weight. Give it another squeeze and mix it with the yoghurt sauce and a splash of olive oil. Garnish with the fresh herbs.

cucumber 1, *peeled and seeded*
salt 1 *tsp*
garlic yoghurt sauce 200 *ml/½ pint (see p200)*
dill or *mint* small bunch, *chopped*

STUFFED PEPPERS
zeytinyağlı biber dolması

It's astonishing to think that the ubiquitous pepper, the very warhorse of colourful Mediterranean cookery, was viewed with suspicion well into the 19th century.

Here's one of the bedrock dishes of the Ottoman region, to serve hot or cold, as a light lunch or a side dish.

- Soak the currants in boiling water for fifteen minutes. Sweat the onion with a splash of olive oil in a pan. As the onion colours, add the sugar, the pine nuts and the drained currants. When the pine nuts start to brown stir in the spices and the rice.
- Cover the rice with water, add a pinch of salt, and simmer for ten minutes or so until it is absorbed.
- Turn off the heat and let the rice steam under a cloth for ten minutes. Add the herbs and stir gently.
- Wash the peppers, slice off their tops, scoop out seeds and strings, and stuff them loosely with the rice mixture. Pop the tops back on and pack the peppers together upright in a saucepan.
- Mix lemon juice, the same amount of olive oil and about 200ml of water in a bowl, pour it over the peppers, and bring the pan to the boil. Clap on a lid and simmer for twenty minutes or so, until the peppers are done.

currants 2 tbsp
onion 1 medium, chopped
olive oil
sugar 1 tsp
pine nuts 3 tbsps
cinnamon 2 tsp
dried mint 1 tsp
allspice ½ tsp
short grain rice 150g/5oz
salt
dill, parsley and *mint* small bunches, finely chopped
peppers 4
juice of a lemon

This is very good with garlicky yoghurt.

In place of short grain rice you could substitute bulgar or even whole wheat: just adjust the timing so that they're done when they go into the peppers.

PRESSED BEEF
pastırma

The Turkish horsemen of Central Asia used to preserve meat in pockets on the sides of their saddles, pressing it with their legs as they rode. Pastırma means 'pressed', and this pressed, dry-cured beef off the steppe is the origin of the Italian pastrami and consequently the mainstay of a thousand New York delis. The best pastırma comes from Kayseri in central Turkey – Evliya Çelebi, the great and witty traveller, recommended it in the 17th century. Most of it is eaten in Istanbul. If you want to have a go making your own, it's not very difficult but requires patience and a fortnight. The best quality pastırma is made with fillet but topside can be used, too. Given the effort, it's worth starting with the very best beef you can afford.

- Trim the fillet to remove any fat, then rinse it and pat it dry. Lay the meat out flat in an earthenware dish and cover it with salt. After four hours or so, rinse the fillet, chuck the salt, and start again. This time, place a layer of greaseproof paper over the top, cover with a board, and weigh the board down with something heavy – a pan of water, a stone, whatever. Put the fillet somewhere cool, or in the fridge.
- Every day, for the next two weeks, pour away the brine formed as the salt draws out the moisture from the beef, and replace with fresh salt.
- Once the salt stays dry, wash it off, and put the fillet in a pan of cold water overnight.
- Next day, pat the beef dry and hang it for a couple of days in a cool, dry place – your larder would be ideal, or a chilly barn, but the porch or a fridge is fine.
- Now make the paste, called çemen, whizzing the remaining ingredients together in a food processor or bashing them in a mortar, then adding water to make a sticky paste.

fillet of beef (or topside) 1kg
plenty of fine sea salt
fenugreek seeds 8 tbsp, ground
red pepper 65g, diced
hot chillies 15g, chopped
garlic cloves 100g/4oz, peeled
cumin 2 tsp, ground

- Work the paste into the meat, coating it entirely. Hang it up again, where the air can get at it – the fenugreek and the garlic seem to stop flies – for 24 hours in hot weather, 2 or 3 days if it's cold. The çemen paste should be tacky, and the meat itself hard, but not without some give when you press it.
- Wrap the pastırma in a cheesecloth and keep it in the fridge. It can be served in very thin slices as a cold hors d'oeuvre, or cooked with eggs and tomatoes. You can eat it on toast or pop it into the bean stew – fasulye – on p190.

PALEWSKI'S BOILED BEEF WITH SORREL SAUCE
wołowina Palewskiego w sosie szczawiowym

The Turks don't eat beef the way they eat lamb: meat, in Turkey, means lamb unless otherwise directed. But the Polish ambassador Palewski, dreaming of his homeland amid the winter snows in Istanbul, thinks of a boiled beef dinner which he would have done like this:

- Put the brisket into a cast iron pot or saucepan, and scald with boiling water, to cover. Add a tsp of salt and simmer for an hour and a half, skimming the broth. Peel the onion, chop it in half, and singe it over a naked flame. Put it into the pot with the other aromatics, and simmer very gently for another hour.
- Clean the sorrel, discarding the stalks, and chop it roughly. Toss it into a frying pan with a little melted butter and the chopped garlic, and stir it until the sorrel goes soft and khaki. Season with salt and pepper, and beat in the cream.
- Serve the beef thickly sliced with the sorrel sauce and potatoes mashed with some of the beef stock.

beef brisket 1kg/2lb
salt
onion 1
leek 1, *chopped in two*
carrots 2, *thickly sliced*
celeriac ½ *small, or two sticks of celery, sliced*
big wedge of savoy cabbage
peppercorns 6
pinch of allspice berries
bayleaf
pepper

For the sauce
bunch of sorrel
butter, 1 tbsp
garlic 1 clove, finely chopped
cream 250ml/1 cup

Beef braised with fennel and garlic
rezene ve sarımsaklı fırnda et

This is a lovely aromatic dish that is as good cold as hot, and cooks quietly, without interference.

- In a casserole with a tight fitting lid, brown the meat in the oil. Add all the other ingredients except the sugar and onions, put the lid on tight and lower the heat of the hob to a whisper.
- After an hour, add the sugar and onions and turn the meat. Replace the lid and cook for another hour, very slowly.
- Serve sliced on a warm plate, drizzled with its juices.

shin of beef 1kg/2lb, boned and rolled
olive oil
fennel seeds 2 tbsp
garlic 2 cloves
wine 2 tsp
water 4 tbsp
splash of olive oil
pearl onions or *small shallots* ½ kg/1lb, peeled
sugar 1 tbsp

POPPY SEED CAKE
haşhaşlı ve damla sakızlı revani

This is a classic Istanbul palace pudding, sweet and soft, with hints of vanilla. You can also add mastic, traditionally brought from the island of Chios, for the scent of Mediterranean pine woods.

- First make the syrup. Bring the sugar and water to the boil, stirring until the sugar melts. Stir for another five minutes while letting the oven heat up to 180°C. Set the syrup aside to cool.
- Pour the sugar into a mixing bowl. Break in the eggs and whisk to a froth. Continue beating as you add the olive oil, then the milk, semolina, flour, baking powder and vanilla. Finally stir in the poppy seeds.
- Grease an 8-inch cake tin and pour in the mixture. Put it in the oven for 45 minutes, until the top browns.
- Remove the cake from the oven, pour the syrup evenly over the surface, and set aside to absorb the syrup while it cools.
- Delicious with cream, or ice cream.

For syrup
granulated sugar *300g/1 cup*
water *375ml/1½ cups*

granulated sugar *200g/1 cup*
eggs *3*
olive oil *230ml/½ pint*
milk *225ml/scant ½ pint*
semolina *180g/6oz*
flour *180g/6oz*
baking powder *1 tbsp*
vanilla extract *1 tbsp*
poppy seeds *145g/5oz*

An Evil Eye

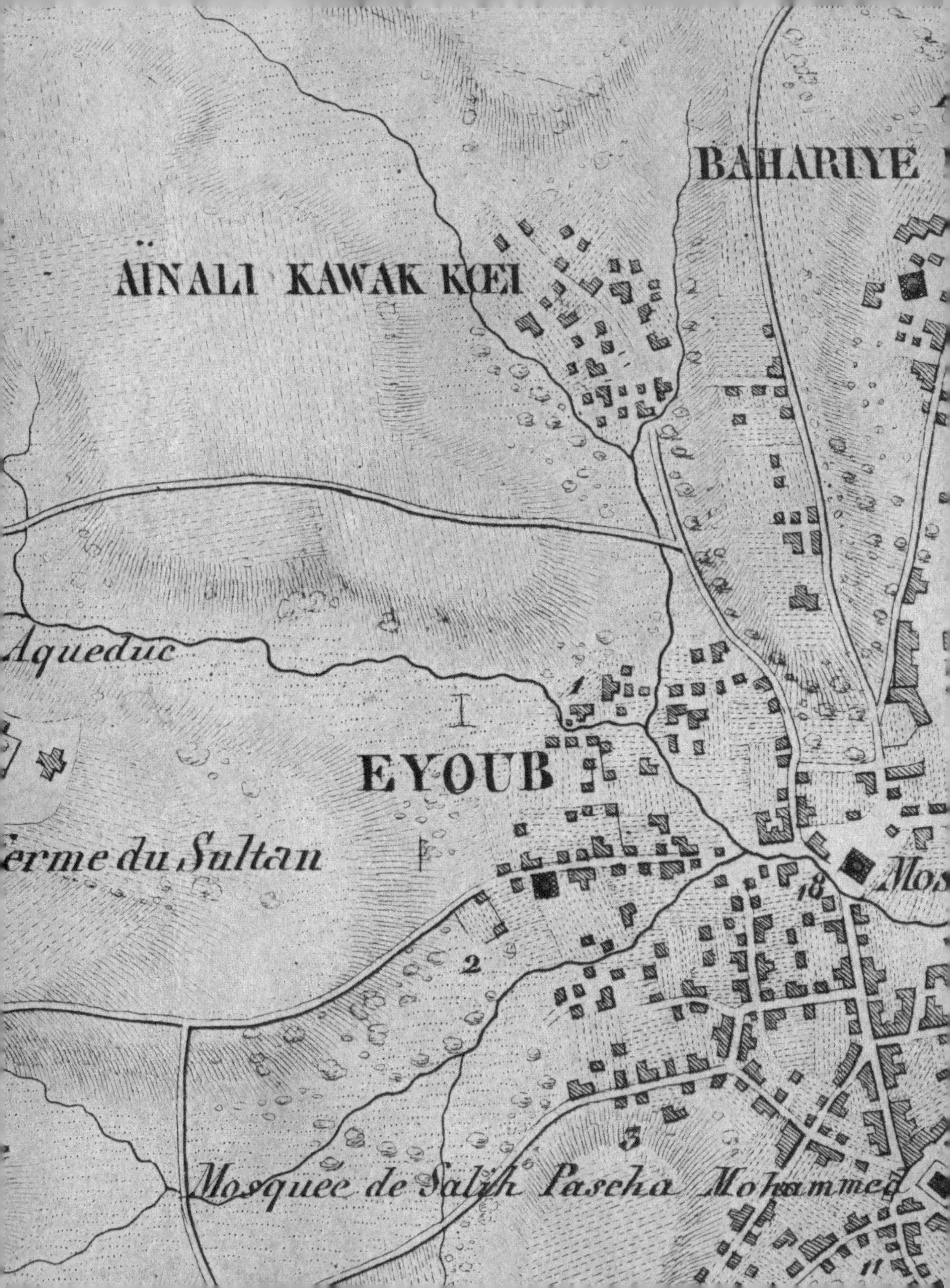

BAHARIYE

AÏNALI KAWAK KŒI

Aqueduc

EYOUB

erme du Sultan

Mos

18

2

3

Mosquee de Salih Pascha Mohammed

11

Les eau

Serai de Kara

Vieille Palce

Reservoir des barques du Sultan

Palais de la Sultane Esma

Palais de la Sultane Khadidje

Palais de la Sult ...gkhan

Cimetiere Grec

SÜDEÜDJE

...beau et ...dation de ...Sult Walide

...standji ...iskelessi

...d'Eyoub

Abord d'Eyoub

Mosquée   Mosquée d'Ahmed Pacha

Mosquée   KHALIDJI-OG

Caserne des Bombardiers

Vieille Fonderie

Yashim's last adventure contains a Polish prince, a band of Italian revolutionaries, a dream of food - and baklava, the quintessential Ottoman treat, still made wherever the horsetail standards flew.

> On Thursdays he went early to market, and bought the finest ingredients his friend George could bring to his stall: tiny aubergines, peppers as long and curled as Turkish slippers, fresh white onions, okra, beans. Later, Palewski would come into the room, sniffing the air, surprising Yashim by his knack for guessing what he'd made for dinner. A chicken, perhaps, Persian style with walnuts and pomegranate juice; mackerel stuffed with nuts and fruits, and grilled; a succession of little meze, soups, dolma, or aromatic rice. Once he had brought a Frenchman to dine with them, too, and as a consequence a man had died – and Stanislaw Palewski had saved Yashim's life.

The Baklava Club

Baklava

Probably no-one makes baklava quite like the guys at Karaköy, who stack them in trays and scoop them up on a slice in serried rows, like regimented dormice, and use walnuts and pistachio and hazelnut and honey which oozes from the base. Which still, inexplicably, stays crisp. What – you prefer the little shop over in Balat? Really? Which just goes to show that it's all a matter of taste.

- Oil the sides and base of a cake tin, round or square-edged.
- Take a sheet of filo, lay it in the tin and push it to the edges. Brush with oil and don't worry that the edges are flopping over the rim, because you can trim them up later.
- Carry on layering and oiling the filo until you've used up half the sheets. Pour the nuts over the top oiled sheet and spread them evenly. Sprinkle with cinnamon and carry on with the filo layers until it's all gone.
- Trim the edges clean with a knife.
- Butter the top layer, press it down with your fingers or a plate, and place in the fridge for an hour, to set.
- Use a sharp knife to cut the slab into diamonds. Make parallel incisions about an inch apart, right through to the base.
- Slide the pan into the oven, preheated to 160°C/325°F, and bake for about an hour, until the top is golden.
- Melt the honey in a pan with the orange peel and half cup of Earl Grey tea. Turn the heat down, stir in the lemon juice and simmer for five minutes. Leave to cool.
- Take out the baklava, pour the cool syrup over it, and allow it to cool.

for 12
olive oil 100g/ ½ cup
filo sheets 250g/8oz
walnuts 225g/7oz, or a
mixture of walnuts, pistachios
and almonds, finely chopped
cinnamon 1 tsp, ground
butter 1 tbsp, melted
Earl Grey tea bag 1
honey 250ml/1 cup
orange peel 1 tbsp
lemon ½

"At the cheesemonger's stall they stopped for a block of salty white *beyaz peynir* made of pure sheep's milk, and a block of stringy *dil peyniri* – 'which is wonderful with pickles,' Yashim explained. 'Come on.'

They crossed the street to an old man with curved moustaches, whose wife's pickles were widely considered to be the best in the market.

'Dil peyniri is good to eat with your fingers. It's mild, and you pull it into strings and wrap the strings around a green pickled tomato and pop it into your mouth.'

They hesitated over the jars of pickles, eventually choosing three of Yashim's favourites: *patlican tursusu*, made of stuffed aubergines; a jar

Of course the real picnic was carried by porters and slaves

of turnips, pickled in grape juice, with a sliver of beetroot thrown in, for the prettiness of its colour; and some long, green chillies.

The basket was almost full, and very heavy.

'We used to picnic on the Black Sea,' Yashim remembered. 'They made me carry a basket, and I always grumbled.'

He smiled, looking back: he could see now that his parents had given him a little basket of his own to help him appreciate the coming feast.

'Of course the real picnic was carried by porters and slaves. Hampers and hampers! Let's get *pastirma*.'

At the meat-stall he bought a pound of the best from Kayseri, made from beef fillet. He explained to Natasha how the meat was pressed, rubbed with *çemen* paste made of fenugreek, garlic and chilli, and then sun-dried.

'Fenugreek?'

'Smell it.'

She did, and pulled a face. They bought a couple of horseshoe shaped rounds of *sucuk*, a dried sausage made of lamb with garlic and cumin, and moved on to buy pistachios and fresh green chillies.

'Do you like caviar?'

'Yashim, you're joking…'

So he bought half a pound of Persian sturgeon's eggs, the black kind, lightly salted in their own purse. 'Try it from the other side of the Caspian,' he remarked. On their way out of the market Yashim stopped a simit seller, and bought a dozen coils of the spiced dry bread from the tray the man carried on his head.

'I think the Validé must be coming after all,' she whispered.

He selected a tray of baklava: 'This,' he said, 'you'll like.' He smiled, thinking of Palewski's joke. 'The Italians love it.' They watched the man lay his selection carefully between thin wooden boards. The man's young son bound the boards together with raffia ribbons, which he tied off and curled with a zip of his fingernail.

Finally, at the apothecary, he bought four ounces of China tea, wrapped in paper.

The basket was so heavy he engaged one of the porters who carried bales and boxes uphill on their backs, secured by a band across their foreheads. He was a stocky man with delicate hands, and he grunted with amusement when he saw Yashim's load.

STUFFED AUBERGINES
imam bayildı

The name of this dish means the Imam fainted. Cookbooks will tell you he swooned at its delicious taste, or the cost of the olive oil. But I think it alludes to the yonic appearance of the split aubergine. Imam Bayildi is very good with an onion-based tomato sauce, but Yashim's version instead uses the pomegranate molasses that tomatoes-with-sugar largely replaced in Mediterranean cooking.

- Melt the onion very gently in olive oil, with the garlic, lemon zest, salt, and cumin, in a pan with a lid on.
- With a peeler half-skin the aubergines in stripes, without cutting off the ends. Slit them from stem to stern, but keeping their hulls watertight by not quite cutting all the way through, to form a pocket. Put them in salty water for twenty minutes, then drain and squeeze.
- Brown them on all sides in a frying pan with oil.
- Lift the lid on the onions. Drizzle them with the molasses and lemon juice. Stir the pan and take it off the heat.
- Open the pockets in the aubergines with your fingers, squeezing the flesh to make the opening large enough to take the onions. Stuff as much of the mixture as you can into each one, and lay them in a saucepan.
- Pour in 100ml water, drizzle with olive oil and the remaining mixture, and bring the water up to the boil. Turn down the heat and barely simmer, with the lid on, for an hour. Baste now and again.
- Serve them cut into thick slices, at room temperature, with oil and lemon wedges.

onions 2, sliced
olive oil 150ml/½ cup
garlic 4 cloves, chopped
lemon 1, zested and squeezed
salt 1 tsp
cumin 1 tsp
aubergines (eggplant) 2 large
pomegranate molasses 2 tbsp
lemon wedges

For a conventional version, chop a couple of tomatoes with 1 tbsp sugar and the onion mix, and stuff the prepared aubergines. Leave out the molasses, and season with dill and parsley, chopped.

"Palewski reached for the barrel and began rubbing it furiously with a rag. 'Boutet, the finest gunmaker in France. Fowling piece. A three foot barrel, and exceptionally light, no? Boutet's genius. I don't suppose Boutet's ever made more than a dozen of these and I've found two in the gun cupboard. If you don't mind getting your hands dirty, you can polish up the other one. Truth is, I'd forgotten all about them. Seen enough guns by 1812 to think they were worth avoiding, I suppose.'

'And now?'

'Now, thanks to Midhat Pasha's invitation, Yashim, I've discovered these beauties. Look at that dolphin on the trigger guard!'

'Midhat Pasha's invitation?'

'Duck. Snipe. Sure you won't take a rag?'

'Midhat Pasha has asked you to go shooting?'

'Wildfowling. We call it wildfowling. I was about to send him my regrets when I remembered the old gun cupboard in the cellar. Marta produced the key.'

"We call it wildfowling"

'And when you opened the cupboard –'

'When I opened the cupboard I found this sublime pair. Someone has left them in a shocking state. There's rust and fouling in the breech of this one, and of course the stocks need oiling.'

Yashim picked up one of the wooden stocks, slim and fine-curled, almost like a bird in flight.

'There are a couple of good gunsmiths in the arms bazaar.'

'I'll see how well I can do first.' Palewski squinted down the barrel. 'This one's barrel seems perfect, but there's something wrong with the firing mechanism.'

Yashim nodded. 'I know the feeling.'

Palewski laughed. Yashim had something wrong with his firing mechanism, too. He was a decade younger than his friend, well-built, dark, with curious grey eyes and a face that lit up with a smile: but Yashim was a eunuch.

WILD DUCK OTTOMAN STYLE
fırında Osmanlı ördeği

Palewski's shoot on the lakes outside Istanbul produced a decent bag and Marta, his housekeeper, would have known what to do with a brace of wild duck.

- Rub the butter over your ducks, with the thyme. Put a few sprigs inside, too.
- Pound the bread in mortar, and soften it with olive oil. With wild duck be generous with the oil; farmed duck is fattier and you will want a drier mixture. Mix in the garlic and the oregano, and stuff the ducks.
- Beat the honey with a little more oil and drizzle it over the ducks. Scatter the giblets and the almonds around the pan and roast the birds for 25 minutes in a hot oven (230°C/450°F/Gas 8), until the skin is brown.
- Serve with pilaf and a salad.

butter 175g/6oz

2 wild or 1 farmed duck, drawn and plucked

thyme small bunch

stale bread 6 slices

olive oil

garlic 4 cloves, crushed

oregano 4 tsp, dried

runny honey 5 tbsp

almonds 5 tbsp blanched

The Baklava Club

PAN FRIED NETTLE WITH CUMIN
ısırgan otu yemeği

Most of us have lost all knowledge of using wild herbs and leaves, which would have been standard in Ottoman times. A patient cook, browsing over a small patch of grassy ground, could fill a basket with edible greens. So let's begin modestly, with nettles.

Pick them early in the year, when the tips are small, avoiding roadsides or anywhere that might have been sprayed. In rubber gloves, pinch off the top five leaves of each plant. At home, wash them thoroughly and pick off as much stem as you wish, like preparing spinach. You could substitute spinach or chard if you can't get the nettles.

- In a frying pan or wok heat the oil, and add the cumin.
- Toss in the nettles. Add salt.
- Stir fry on a hot heat for three to five minutes.

olive oil 1 tbsp

cumin seeds 1 tsp

nettles 100g/3oz, rinsed and drained

salt 1 tsp

The nettles are very good sprinkled over a plain pilaf.

BEAN STEW
kuru fasulye

John and Berrin Scott, who produce the world's best magazine, *Cornucopia*, took me into the Belgrade Forest to see the reservoirs built by Sinan to supply Istanbul with fresh water. On the way we pulled into a village in the hills where they had heard of a good place to eat. It was a sort of truck stop, and we ordered *kuru fasulye*, as John and Berrin always do, looking for the very best. White beans, *fasulye*, are the base food of Turkey, its pasta or potato – what my mother referred to as the padding. In Italian, they are called *fasoglio*.

- Soak the beans overnight. Boil in fresh water until tender. Or use the pressure cooker.
- Soften the onion in olive oil in a big pan over medium heat. Add the garlic, cumin and the aubergine, and fry until the aubergine is soft. Stir in the pepper, add the isot biber, the sugar and a sprinkling of salt and pepper, and after a minute pour the tomatoes into the pan. Crush them up if they're whole.
- Simmer for twenty minutes, uncovered, then add the beans with a decent splash of the cooking water, and stir.
- Simmer for another fifteen minutes to let the beans absorb the flavours, and serve with plain rice and the quick pickle on p149.

butter beans 500g/1lb, soaked and boiled
onion 1, chopped
glug of olive oil
garlic 3–4 cloves, chopped
cumin seeds ½ tsp
aubergine 1 medium, diced
red pepper 1, finely sliced
isot biber 1 tsp
sugar ½ tbsp
salt and pepper
tomatoes 1 tin (400g/14oz)

" The juice of the grated courgettes looked like jade in the bowl. He lit a fire in the grate, sprinkled it with charcoal, and set a pan to boil. With a sharp knife he peeled the celeriac, chopped it into small cubes and dropped the pieces into the water, with the artichokes.

The pan was boiling: he skinned a dozen small onions and blanched them.

'I like to watch you work,' Natasha said.

He had almost forgotten her sitting on the divan.

'Tell me about Siberia. Tell me about your home.'

He worked while she talked. He put carrots, onions, artichokes and celeriac into a bigger saucepan, with a sprig of thyme and a bay leaf, and covered them all with stock.

'We used to pretend we were really in St Petersburg. Sergei had money – they didn't confiscate his estates, I don't know why – and he had an opera house built in Irkutsk. We sewed our own clothes, but we threw balls, proper dances, with an orchestra. Everyone always wanted to believe that we would go home. The children were brought up knowing how to behave.'

Yashim broke two eggs into a bowl with a cup of flour and beat them together. He gave the courgettes a final squeeze and mixed them in. On the board he chopped onions, with a handful of dill and parsley, and pounded some garlic in the mortar with a pinch of salt. He swept it all into the courgette mixture, and stirred it round. Finally he set an open pan on the heat, and threw in butter and olive oil.

"He had an opera house built in Irkutsk"

'Some did,' Natasha went on. 'One by one, the families left. We used to give them a ball on the night of their departure. The boys who were leaving would ask the girls who were staying for the first dance...'

Her voice trailed off.

The butter was bubbling. Yashim began to drop spoonfuls of the courgette mix into the pan: they spread and blossomed as they fell.

COURGETTE FRITTERS
mücver

The perfect picnic food, prepared in advance.

- Grate the courgettes, skin and all, into a colander. Mix them around with a teaspoonful of salt and let them drain for half an hour under a plate weighted down with something heavy – a pan of water will do.

- Squeeze the courgettes again, to help expel their water, which is a beautiful jade green in the bowl. The drier the better. In a bowl, mix them with the garlic and onion, sprinkle with pul biber and a scrunch of black pepper, and crumble the feta into the mix. Stir in the egg yolk and the flour. Beat the egg white into foam, and fold it gently into the mix.

- Cover the bottom of a shallow frying pan with sunflower oil on a medium to hot stove. When the oil begins to flex, drop dollops of the mixture into the pan with a wooden spoon or your fingers. They may be about three inches across; give them a nudge here and there to improve their shape while they are still soft. Pat them down a bit if you like.

- Fry for three minutes on one side, then turn them carefully with a spatula and fry the other side. Lift them out and put them on kitchen paper to dry off, then start again with another glug of oil until you have used up all the mixture.

courgettes 2

salt

garlic 2 cloves, finely chopped

onion 1, grated

pul biber or chilli flakes pinch

pepper

feta cheese 1 tbsp

egg 1, yolk and white separated

flour 1 tbsp

sunflower oil 200ml/½ cup

Çusla, ou grand cuisinier d'un régiment de Janni-
saires.

The Baklava Club

CARROT AND BEETROOT FRITTERS
havuc ve pancar kizartması

These are prepared the same way as the courgette fritters on the previous page, but a grated potato well tossed with the other ingredients provides the starch that holds everything together. If they take a minute longer to cook their colour is glorious, imperial purple, like the buskins of a Byzantine despot.

- Mix the grated vegetables together in a colander, squeezing to expel water.
- In a bowl mix them with the cumin and garlic, salt, pepper and pul biber.
- Stir in the egg yolk. Beat the egg white into foam, and fold it gently into the mix.
- Cover the bottom of a shallow frying pan with sunflower oil on a medium to hot stove. When the oil begins to flex, drop dollops of the mixture into the pan with a wooden spoon or your fingers. They may be about two inches across; give them a nudge here and there to improve their shape while they are still soft. Pat them down a bit if you like.
- Fry for three minutes on one side, then turn them carefully with a spatula and fry the other side. Lift them out and put them on kitchen paper to dry off, then start again with another glug of oil until you have used up all the mixture.
- Eat them right away, with yoghurt sauce (see p200).

carrots 3, *peeled and grated*
beetroots 3, *peeled and grated*
potato 1 *medium sized, parboiled and grated*
cumin 1 *tsp, ground*
garlic 2 *cloves*
salt
pepper
pul biber or *chilli flakes* *pinch*
egg 1, *yolk and white separated*
sunflower oil 200 *ml/½ cup*

The Baklava Club

"Yashim turned back to the kitchen. He added charcoal to the fire, put on a pan, and rolled in a couple of lamb shanks, with a short drip of olive oil, to brown. Now and then he gave the pan a violent shake.

He took the pen and on a second sheet of paper wrote down everything he had learned about the attack.

He glanced at the shanks, gave them another shake, and peeled an onion, chopping it fine. Holding the lamb back with a wooden spoon, he poured the fat into a bowl, then dropped a knob of butter between the shanks. It sizzled and he added the onions.

He reached out for various small pots and took a couple of cinnamon sticks, a few cloves, and a big pinch of salt. He pounded peppercorns and allspice berries into his mortar, and scraped them

A ladleful of water calmed the pot

up and stirred them into the pan. They began to catch. A ladleful of water calmed the pot. He added a scattering of sugar.

From a flat basket on the side he selected four plump pomegranates, halved them on a board, and scraped the jeweled seeds into the mortar using a metal spoon. It was a fiddly job. He added a little more water to the pan, crushed the seeds under the pestle, poured the dark, tangy juice into the pan, gave it all a stir, and clapped on the lid. He moved the pan slightly off the coals, and went back to his paper, wiping his hands.

LAMB SHANKS WITH QUINCE
ayva yahnisi

'Eating the quince', in Turkish, means having a tough time: they are not to be taken lightly raw. But cooked – in marmalades, too – they are delicious; as fruit they are beautiful to look at and smell divine. In Istanbul they are sold by men who carry them in baskets on their backs, and wander the streets in the deep winter snows.

- Brown the shanks in oil over a low heat for 20 minutes. Pour off the fat, drop in the butter, let it melt, and add the onion. When it has softened, fling in all the spices except the ground cinnamon, along with the pomegranate molasses, a cup of water, pepper, salt and half the sugar. Give the pan a stir and set it to simmer gently with a lid on for an hour and a half. If the steam escapes, add a little more water.
- Set the pan aside but keep it warm. Pour about half a cupful of the cooking liquid into a frying pan, add the rest of the sugar and the cinnamon, and bring to a smart boil. Drop in the quince pieces and glaze them on both sides as the liquid reduces.
- You can pull the meat off the bones meanwhile, if you want.
- When the quinces are shining with the glaze, tip them and any remaining sauce over the lamb, deglaze the pan with lemon juice and add to the main dish.

lamb shanks 4
olive oil
butter 50g/2oz
onion 1 large, finely chopped
cinnamon 2 sticks
cloves 3
allspice ½ tsp, ground
pomegranate molasses 3 tbsp
pepper
salt
brown sugar 4 tbsp
cinnamon 1 tsp, ground
quinces 4, cored and quartered
juice of a lemon

The Baklava Club

> Answers, decisions, ulcers.

And now all he had to fear was death, which comes to everyone. All he had to do was wait. No calls, no salvers, no letters. Not a care in the world.

He lay back and rubbed his stomach. For the next hour he amused himself, and tortured himself, by making an inventory of the finest breakfasts he had ever eaten. That done, he set to thinking about the food he had left untouched. White butter subsiding into the heart of a warm roll, condemned by a scrumpled napkin. A dish of eggs *en cocotte* that he had once petulantly mashed and sent back, cold, to the kitchen. Silver dishes of deviled kidneys, of crêpes so buttery they glistened over the tiny spirit lamp that chafed the dish; mounds of fresh croissants, baskets overflowing with brioches, baguettes whiter than the snow in Warsaw, or the inside of a redhead's thigh!

Prince Czartoryski dreams of luxury

Baguettes whiter than the snow in Warsaw, or the inside of a redhead's thigh!

Ah! He began to compile a list of all the beauties he had kissed, had flirted with, had actually come to grips with—lots. Polish, Russian, German, French, parlourmaids and duchesses. He thought of them all, and began to pile them up, like brioches, in his mind—mounds of sugary girls, their breasts as white as confectioners' paste, all limbs and dimples and . . .

He stretched and the straw crackled underneath him.

OMLETTE
omlet

Yashim has *börek* for breakfast, but a spicy *omlet* makes a good alternative: or it's lunch. Yashim has made it late at night for a hungry lover. At fancy Istanbul hotels, the breakfast chef will make up your omlet to your liking, and cook it for you on the spot. Two minutes.

- Beat the eggs with the salt and pepper. Melt the butter in a wide frying pan and add the onions just before the butter starts to burn. Stir them about for a few moments, to wilt, then give the pan a shake and pour in the egg. Sprinkle the cooking egg with parsley and chilli, to taste.
- Keep tipping the pan to give the runny egg a chance to slide onto the hot sides. When the parsley is about to be gripped by the setting egg, slip your spatula under the omlet and fold it neatly over. Give it a shake, and serve.

For two
eggs 4
salt
pepper
butter 1 tsp
spring onions 3, sliced in rings, *green parts too*
parsley small bunch, finely chopped
chilli flakes

Garlic yoghurt sauce
sarımsaklı yoğurt

The great French chef Escoffier became famous for establishing five mother sauces to be used in his Victorian kitchens – *Tomate, Béchamel, Velouté, Espagnole,* and *Hollandaise.*
There are a number of mother sauces in Turkish cooking, too. One, made with yoghurt, is essentially a garnish, which takes seconds to make and transports the dullest boiled vegetable to Topkapi Palace. It's good on pilafs, vegetables, salads (try it with raw grated beetroot), and lamb dishes and, without the garlic, it makes a delicious refreshing drink, too.

- Beat the yoghurt in a bowl with the garlic, a pinch of salt, and a splash of cold water. That's it. Did you wish for more?
- Very well: it's up to you to play with the other ingredients. A squeeze of lemon juice adds sharpness. The water simply alters the consistency – you might want a very thin, runny sauce to dress a bowl of salad leaves (purslane is traditional), or a more meaty dollop to cool down a spicy kebab. It's up to you whether you want mintiness, too.

Greek yoghurt 250g/8oz
garlic 1 clove, squashed, peeled and finely chopped with a pinch of salt
water 50ml/4 tbsp
lemon juice
mint 1tsp, fresh or dried

Ayran, the yoghurt drink that everyone drinks with food in Turkey, is made of yoghurt, a pinch of salt, and cold water, beaten together. Whisk it to a foamy beaker of vitality.

LABNE

Not quite cheese, but no longer yoghurt, labne is profoundly Ottoman in its simplicity and versatility. It crops up all across the region once governed from Istanbul, as a side dish, a condiment, a sweet pudding, breakfast food, a dip, or a spicy relish, and when you have made it once you will make it forever.

Labneh is nothing more than yoghurt drained of its whey. To eat it with nuts, stewed fruit and/or honey as a pudding or for breakfast, simply drain the yoghurt plain, overnight, and leave out the other ingredients.

- Beat the yoghurt with the oil and lemon juice, and the garlic if you want, and spoon it into a muslin draped in a colander, or a jam muslin bag, suspended over a bowl to catch the whey.
- Drained overnight, your labne will turn out onto a plate firm but spreadable. If you carry on draining it in the fridge for another day or two it will become quite solid and you can pat and roll it into little walnut sized balls, for keeping in a jar covered with olive oil. Season the oil beforehand with pepper and a handful of chopped herbs – tarragon, parsley, and chives. Let it marinade for a day, and for up to two weeks.

Greek yoghurt 500g/1lb
olive oil 1 tbsp
lemon juice 1 tbsp
garlic 1 clove, crushed and chopped fine with a pinch of salt (optional)

Simple, and chic.

TOMATO SAUCE
sarımsaklı domates sosu

Every child should know how to make tomato sauce. It is cheap, quick, delicious and open to all possible variations. Tinned tomatoes, which look fabulous and taste unbearably sour, are transformed in a few moments into a rich, succulent sauce that can amiably accompany almost anything.

- Empty the tomatoes into a pan. If they are whole, squash them between your fingers or, if you are fussy or very smartly dressed, crush them with a wooden spoon. Put the pan on the heat and stir in the oil, the garlic, the sugar and the salt.
- Bring the tomatoes to the boil then put on a lid and simmer for twenty minutes or more.

tomatoes 400g/14oz tin
generous glug of olive oil
garlic 4–5 cloves, peeled
sugar 1 tsp
salt
herbs and spices a choix

That's the straight version, a perfect sauce, but of course you can enliven it in countless ways. You might, for instance, enlarge it by sweating chopped onions, and maybe a chopped stick of celery, in oil as a base on which to create the sauce as above. You might simply add a bay leaf at the start, or a raft of warm herbs like basil or oregano – but not mint, which would be horrible. A spike of rosemary is ok, but more makes bitter. And you can spice it how you like, with a half teaspoonful of ground cumin, and/or chilli flakes. If you have some leftover stock, add that and leave the lid off for a while.

I don't think it is superior made with fresh tomatoes. If you have a glut, and they are ripe and delicious, make a lighter sauce instead that emphasizes their freshness:

FRESH TOMATO SAUCE
taze domates sosu

- Chop the tomatoes on a board, and sprinkle them with a little salt. Toss the chopped garlic into a frying pan covered with a layer of hot oil. Tilt the board covered in tomatoes to let any water run off into the sink, or a bowl, and sweep them into the pan as the garlic softens, but before it has coloured.
- Stir fry the tomatoes for a moment longer, and that's your sauce. You can add more olive oil.

fresh tomatoes ½ *kg*
salt
garlic 4–5 *cloves, peeled*
generous glug of olive oil

"The cook laid four skewers on the grill, jostled some others into better position, and whipped out three plates, which he began to pile with bunches of coriander and parsley.

Yashim and Natasha eat kebab

'Fresh salad! Fresh for you,' he declared cheerfully, putting an onion on his block. With a dozen swift strokes he reduced the onion to dice, and swept them onto a plate. He split a lemon, drizzled it over the onion, and then scattered the plate with a handful of kirmizi biber, toasted pepper flakes.

Yashim and Natasha watched quietly as their meal was assembled—the salad, the herbs, the tender pieces of lamb liver, the huge blanket of bread, thin as cotton and supple as fine leather, the ayran, a soothing yogurt drink. The liver was the speciality of the house—that is, there was no other: no lamb, no shawarma, no kofta, just liver, cut small and cooked with a hint of smoke.

The man's working rhythm soothed Yashim: it was part efficiency and part show, to reassure them and

Yashim began tearing at the thin bread

other passersby that the cookery was swift and well rehearsed. The plates came swooping to their table: the lamb, still sizzling on its spit, across a plate. Yashim began tearing at the thin bread, choosing morsels of meat and herbs, adding a pinch of onion, dabbing the little parcel into a dish of spicy red pepper flakes.

Natasha watched him.

'You eat too fast.'

Yashim considered this. 'I'm sorry. It's force of habit,' he admitted. 'On the street, at least, I take my rhythm from the cook.'

'He's fast.'

'And methodical.'

Natasha wrapped a morsel of lamb the size of a hazelnut in a sheet of bread and put it in her mouth.

'You forgot the salad.'

She nodded with her mouth full, and almost laughed.

LAMB KEBAB
şiş kebab

Effortless, really, and classic, these kebabs are best grilled over a mass of hot charcoal. If you are using bamboo skewers, soak them for half an hour first.

- Grate the onions into a colander set over a bowl, sprinkle with salt, and leave to sweat for twenty minutes. Press the onions down with a spoon to extract all the juice, chuck the pulp and mix the juice with the garlic and the cumin seeds.
- Stir in the lamb and marinade at room temperature for a few hours, then thread the meat onto skewers.
- Sprinkle the pitta breads with water, and grill them on both sides for a minute.
- Grill the meat for two to three minutes on each side.
- Pop meat, onion and parsley into the bread, with a squeeze of lemon, and eat with both hands.

onions 2
salt 1tsp
garlic 2-3 cloves, crushed
cumin seeds small handful, roasted and crushed
boned shoulder of lamb 1kg/2lb, cut into inch cubes
pitta bread
red onion, sliced
flatleaf parsley, chopped
lemon wedges

The Baklava Club

CHICKPEAS
narlı nohut

A basic pressure cooker reduces the preparation time to an hour and a half. Otherwise you tend to discover that you should have started yesterday.

Without a pressure cooker, soak the chickpeas in cold water overnight, or for at least six hours. Bring them to the boil in fresh water and boil, covered, until tender. The pressure cooker method is to cover them with boiling water, stand for an hour, then cook for half an hour in fresh water.

- Sweat the onion in oil until soft. Stir in half the garlic, crushed and chopped with a generous pinch of salt. Slice the carrot diagonally into thick strips and when it begins to sweat, add the chopped zest of half a lemon, the cumin and the two kinds of chilli flakes. Stir them in. Finally, scatter the sofritto with the rest of the garlic, peeled but whole.
- Drain the chickpeas, leaving a little water at the bottom.
- Once the lemony aroma starts to rise, stir in the tomato paste and the pomegranate molasses, let them meld for a few minutes, and pour in the chickpeas. Stir, and make everything relax with a big splash of stock, chickpea water if you have it, or plain water (I have used homemade apple juice with good effect). Fork out the carrot strips and throw them away: their job is done.
- Squeeze half a lemon over the pan, stir all the ingredients together, add more water, oil or salt to taste, and simmer for ten minutes or so, for the chickpeas to absorb the flavours.
- This can be served with meat, with rice, with a yoghurt sauce (see p200). Give it another squeeze of lemon when you bring it to the table, and a sprinkling of chopped parsley.

onion 1, *chopped*
olive oil
garlic 1 *head*
salt
carrot 1
lemon 1
cumin seeds 1 *tsp*
isot biber ½ *tsp*
a sprinkling of pul biber or *hot chilli flakes*
tomato paste or puree 2 *tbsp*
pomegranate molasses 1 *tbsp*
chickpeas 500g/1lb, *soaked and boiled*
stock or water 200ml/½ *pint*
parsley

Hummus

Like tapas, meze are the civilized accompaniment to drinks – the raki of the Turks, the ouzo of the Greeks, the arak of the Lebanese. The best meze can be simple cucumbers dipped in salt, or grilled and battered sardines, or a bowl of almonds. The point is to serve something fresh and seasonal, to delight the palate. Hummus is always good, to eat with bread or sliced raw vegetables.

- Whizz up all the ingredients except the hot pepper in a blender, with 100ml of the chickpea water. You can also make this in a pestle and mortar, garlic first, then the chickpeas, then the other ingredients.
- The isot biber is for sprinkling on top.

chickpeas 200g/8oz, soaked and boiled
garlic 2 cloves, crushed with 1 tsp salt
tahini 3 tbsp
olive oil 2 tbsp
lemon juice 4 tbsp
cumin seeds ½ tsp
isot biber ½ tsp

ACKNOWLEDGEMENTS

This book could not have been written without the enthusiastic encouragement of Yashim's readers around the world. They called for this book, and here it is.

Isaac Goodwin created it. Clive Crook provided the initial impetus, suggesting a master design which Isaac adapted and reinterpreted, tirelessly sifting the text, the artwork and the layout to produce a book which is, I hope, as good to read and look at as to work from. Isaac has been a patient and inspired collaborator throughout.

I've been lucky to have detailed editing input from not one, but two of the greatest living cookbook editors, on either side of the Atlantic. In the UK Anne Furniss, the former CEO of Quadrille Books, and in the US Sheilah Kaufman, co-founder of Cookbook Construction Crew. Sheilah is also the award-winning author, with Nur Ilkin, of The Turkish Cookbook: Regional Recipes and Stories. Her knowledge is encyclopaedic and her generosity quite outstanding.

While the recipes are firmly rooted in the soil of the eastern Mediterranean – with a brief foray to the Veneto, and another into the grasslands of Poland – they have been cooked and approved around the world by Yashim fans, who volunteered to try out all the dishes. From Albania to Alabama, Pakistan to Pinner, Amina Beres, Ann Barnes, Ann Bloxwich, Ann Chandonnet, Ann Elizabeth Robinson, Anthea Simmons, Beth Bandy, Beverly Firme, Bill Bosies, Britta de Graaff, Burcak Gurun Muraben, Carey Combe, Carmen Mahood, Carol Titley, Catherine Johnson, Chloe Potts, Claire Byrne, Clare Hogg (of the blog Saucy Dressings), Connie Hay, Daemon A. 'Bunny' Condie, David Lee Tripp, Diana Moores, Dianne Hennessy King, Donna Cummings, Dr Werner and Sonja Keck of Heidelberg, Eva Krygier, Evren Işınak Bruce, Francine Berkowitz, Rev. Fr. Gary Simpson, Genia Ruland, Geoff Perriman, Giles Milton, Giuseppe Mancini, Greg Burrows, Hira Najam in Pakistan, Indrek Koff, Irena Rywacka, Ivette Buere Cantu, Ivor Gethin, Jan Suermondt, Jean Stearns, Jeanette Kearney, Jill Patience, Jillian Wilkinson, Judith O'Hagan, Juliet Emerson, Kate Hubbard, Leary Hasson, Lennart Allen, Linda Gunderson, Lynda Dagdeviren, Maria Figueroa Küpçü, Mark Culme-Seymour, Marsha Frazier, Marta Bialon, Matthew Adams, Meg Officer, Melanie Ulrich, Olivia Temple, Pat Ruttum, Penny Harvey, Piret Frey, Rick Page, Robin Morris, The Rev. Roger Russell, Ron Garrison of Denver, Colorado, Rosemary Petersen, Russell Needham, Ruth Peers, Sally Catton, Sid Cumberland, Simon Allen, Sophie Ransom, Stella Ruland, Stuart MacBride, Sue Aysan, Susan Dolinko, Suzi Clarkson (an English expat in Sarıyer, Muğla, Turkey), Tomas

Eriksson of Malmo, and Veronica and Alfio Brivio followed my recipes and gave me invaluable feedback. Yashim Cooks Istanbul simply could not have happened without their help.

The really beautiful photographs on pages 25, 38-39, 43, 64-65, 66, 90, 94, 99, 153, 160 and 207 are the work of Tuba Şatana, whose website www.istanbulfood.com is an unparalleled guide to the food and culture of Istanbul and Turkey. Tuba is a mine of information and also a lot of fun: if you're planning a visit to the city, you should get in touch with her first.

I photographed the food. Other images come from our own collection, including the map of Constantinople.

I should like to thank my family, who have been so tolerant of this obsession, especially Kate with her wise suggestions and advice, and Harry with his masterly film editing.

INDEX

Entries in italics denote book extracts

Page numbers in italics denote an illustration

ABOUT THE AUTHOR

Jason Goodwin first reached Istanbul in 1990, after covering two thousand miles on foot across Eastern Europe. His account of that journey, On Foot to the Golden Horn, won the John Llewellyn Rhys prize. He went on to write Lords of the Horizons: A History of the Ottoman Empire.

Dmitri Kotjuh

Jason's detective hero, Yashim, operates in the historic Istanbul of 1836-42. His five adventures have been bestsellers around the world. The Janissary Tree won the coveted Edgar Allen Poe Award for Best Novel in 2007 and books in the series have been translated into 40 languages.

Non-fiction:
The Gunpowder Gardens: Travels in China and India in Search of Tea
On Foot to the Golden Horn: A Walk to Istanbul
Lords of the Horizons: A History of the Ottoman Empire
Greenback: The Almighty Dollar and the Invention of America

Yashim the Ottoman Investigator novels:
The Janissary Tree
The Snake Stone
The Bellini Card
An Evil Eye
The Baklava Club

Find out more at www.jasongoodwin.info

Published in Great Britain
in 2016 by Argonaut Books

ISBN 9780957254015

Printed and bound in China by C&C Offset

Designed by Isaac Goodwin
www.isaacgoodwin.com

www.jasongoodwin.info